MY FAVOURITE
CRICKETER

MY FAVOURITE
CRICKETER

EDITED BY JOHN STERN

First published in the UK in 2010 by
A & C Black Publishers Ltd
36 Soho Square, London W1D 3QY
www.acblack.com

ISBN 978 1 4081 2340 9

This book is produced using paper that is made from wood grown in
managed, sustainable forests. It is natural, renewable and recyclable.
The logging and manufacturing processes conform to the
environmental regulations of the country of origin.

Typeset in Minion Pro by Palimpsest Book Production Limited,
Grangemouth, Stirlingshire

Printed and bound in China by Leo Paper Products Ltd

CONTENTS

INTRODUCTION

Hero worship takes many forms. Some love larger than life, as Bonnie Tyler sang, others prefer "honest and modest", as Peter Roebuck says of Harold Larwood. Some are wowed by raw talent or seduced by beauty and flair. There are the imitators and the obsessives, the autograph hunters and the wannabes, finding heroism or idolatry in the underdog or the lame duck.

They are all in this book. This is an assortment of cricket essays, compiled from *The Wisden Cricketer* magazine's 'My Favourite Cricketer' series, which has run every month since early 2005. The idea for the feature is sadly not my own but that of my friend and colleague Sambit Bal, the editor of the world's leading cricket website Cricinfo.com, who kicked off the series in the now defunct *Wisden Asia Cricket* magazine.

It is a simple concept that offers endless variety. The players selected range from the all-time global icons to the self-effacing, small-town hero. Sometimes these apparently contradictory archetypes merge into one, such as Frank Keating's Tom Graveney or Gillian Reynolds' Brian Statham.

The writers are also an assortment: journalists, broadcasters, cricketers, critics, novelists, actors and so on. All they have in common is a love of cricket and an ability to articulate it. There are those who observe from afar; there are childhood obsessions; some have subsequently met their heroes; for a few this has been an adulthood admiration, a rekindling or reassessment of childhood passions.

As much as this book is about hero worship, it is about inspiration. It is about the reasons and the circumstances in which people came to fall in love with cricket. "The first time is always the best," writes the aforementioned Keating, whose luscious prose has adorned the pages of *The Guardian* for decades.

One of cricket's many unique qualities is its ability to reveal personality. The length and pace of the game (even its shortest format) and the individual battles within a team context create an environment in which spectators, either at the ground or on television, can feel uncommonly close to the participants. And of course this proximity creates bonds, whether they be of curiosity, affection, disenchantment or simply a sense of feeling that one knows the players.

A five-day Test can stretch over 30 hours' playing time if it goes its full distance, which is an awfully long time for 22 individuals to be in the public gaze. And even when a player is not actually on the field, he might be waiting to bat and at many grounds visible to the audience, especially so on television. So every emotion, every personality quirk, every mundane tic or affectation is exposed to the watching public.

It is this apparent accessibility, and indeed vulnerability, of cricketers – even today in the ultra-professional and protective age – that captures our hearts and minds so readily. And so we are drawn in and before we know it we are hooked.

John Stern
Editor, *The Wisden Cricketer*
www.thewisdencricketer.com

WASIM AKRAM
by MIKE SELVEY

Illusions of grandeur

Mike Selvey on the Pakistani whose sleight of bowling hand delivered magic and trapped a hundred batsmen leg-before

It must have been late August 11 years ago when Wasim Akram sent down what remains the most amazing delivery I have witnessed in half a century of watching and playing cricket. I say witnessed but that would be overstating things, rather like saying we have seen with our own eyes the illusionist David Copperfield make the Statue of Liberty disappear.

What the Test-match crowd at The Oval that day saw – or we thought we saw – defeated the naked eye, a sleight of hand so fast that it fooled batsman, umpire, fielders, press-box, spectators and, until a replay in very slow motion revealed all, television commentators and audience as well. And from it no wicket resulted, no run accrued. The scorebook will show another dot, with perhaps a scribbled aside that Akram's vehement lbw appeal was dismissed by Merv Kitchen or BC Cooray (I cannot for the life of me remember which) as if scarcely worthy of consideration.

Robert Croft was the England batsman and even he may not recall the incident. As was Wasim's wont late in an innings, when the lower order was in and he was striving to finish things off and get back to the dressing room, he was pitter-pattering menacingly in from round the wicket to the right-hander, intent on hooping the ball into hapless leaden feet at a pace hovering around the 90s. At this stage in the innings there was reverse swing too and no bowler was better at exploiting it.

> The sinuous delivery defeated not
> just the batsman but the eye
> and reflex of the umpire

This one went too much, though, we all saw that. From the hand it was directed at leg stump but swung further towards the leg side and on the full too. Croft saw runs, shifted his weight on to his front foot planted just in front of the crease and shaped to leg-glance an easy boundary. He missed, the ball struck his pad on the full halfway between instep and knee roll, Wasim roared and knowingly we chuckled at the impudence of such a frivolous appeal.

What followed set me agape. Here was a replay intending to show the ridiculous nature of the appeal; instead it revealed a feat unparalleled in my experience. The ball left Wasim's hand and before it was midway down the pitch, and already on a considerable angle, it began to shape further towards the leg side. Croft registered this much.

But then, in perhaps the last 15 feet of its traverse from hand to pad, the ball changed direction and began to leave the batsman, straightening down the line of the stumps until it was able to slide past the closed face of Croft's glancing bat and cannon into his front pad bang in front of middle stump. It was as out as an lbw could possibly be but so late had the movement been, and so rapid, that this sinuous delivery had defeated not just the batsman but the eye and reflex of the umpire. Fluke? What does it matter. For the fraction of a second that this took, belief was suspended.

But that was Waz. Throughout his distinguished career the master manipulator was without question my favourite cricketer. Even as I write this there is a photograph to hand of him crouched down with an arm round our first Labrador, which we named after him. His status as the finest left-arm pace bowler of all time surely brooks no argument even in a thin field. His record in Test matches or in the varying shades of green in one-day cricket is remarkable (414 wickets in the former, 502 in the latter), the more so for a fast bowler.

For a considerable period, until the relentless number of matches played by the great spinners of the modern era saw it obliterated, the most frequent entry on a Test scorecard, aside from "run out", was "lbw Akram", with 119 batsmen falling in that manner. ("b Muralitharan" surpassed it, reaching 153, with "lbw Kumble" next on 141.) He and his brother-in-arms Waqar Younis formed the most prolific opening attack the game has seen, with 497 victims from matches in which they opened together, though this fails to tell the complete story: as opening bowlers they were good but with the old ball they were peerless.

His yorker
was as devastating
as any

His achievement goes beyond statistics, though, and into the realms of charisma and excitement, natural skill. He could bowl fast, nastily so, with the fastest arm in the business, a whiplash that by rights ought to have cracked as he let the ball go. But he could throttle back too, working the ball with wrist and fingers, and at his best he had a total control over length and direction. His yorker, especially that toe-cruncher from round the wicket, was as devastating as any.

Put simply he could do things with the ball, old or new (scuffed sometimes, maybe, but knowing how to use it to best advantage was still a skill in its own right), of which no one else was capable. He could reverse-swing both ways (even in the same delivery, as we have seen) and few have been able to do that. At Melbourne in the World Cup final of 1992 he knocked the stuffing out of England with successive deliveries, naturally from around the wicket. The first, to Allan Lamb, snaked away and bowled him off-stump outside his bat. The next, to Chris Lewis, careered inside a probing blade and took middle. Wasim, his lime-green shirt fluorescent under the lights, screamed and danced his adrenal celebrations. It was spectacular, the mark of genius.

MIKE SELVEY played three Tests for England and is cricket correspondent of *The Guardian*

MIKE ATHERTON
by EMMA JOHN

A man defined by stubbornness

**Emma John's teenage years were not consumed by boy bands.
She went crazy for Athers, dirty pockets and all**

I am too young to feel nostalgic about anything to do with English cricket. The only 'good old days' I long to return to are the Edgbaston and Trent Bridge Tests of 2005 and, thanks to the DVD box set, I can indulge that wish in private. I grew up with the Atherton years and I would not wish to relive them, that mid-1990s period when England had a 50% failure rate in Test series. Most of us could barely watch them the first time round.

Yet, whatever Freddies or Dazzlers you try to woo me with, my heart will remain stubbornly loyal to Michael Andrew Atherton, a man defined by stubbornness. Brainy, patently talented, boyishly attractive, he offered several compelling reasons for following his career – and by extension Lancashire – before his prophesied, yet sudden, ascent to the England captaincy in the charred remains of the 1993 Ashes. In his second Test, aged 25, he pulled off a miracle win at The Oval. Even Geoffrey Boycott might have had a crush on him that day. I had never been one for boy bands but that last-hour, last-wicket thrill was my first experience of teen hysteria.

Among the many things I loved about the baby-faced Mancunian were his crisp defensive shots, the way the bat dropped so perfectly down behind the ball like the needle on kitchen scales. But the quality for which I really adored him was the one that drove so many to distraction – mulishness, obduracy, bloody-mindedness, call it what you like; it was the quality that served as England's spine for each of his 52 Tests as captain and another 36 after he resigned. In the opening Test of his first tour in charge, against West Indies, he showed exactly what kind of leader he would be, taking Courtney Walsh's firebolts literally on the chin and facing down Curtly Ambrose's death-glares with an impish grin.

That was how he inspired his team, and, whatever their performances, he did inspire them. He inspired me, too. Whether the team were having a good day or more often a bad, the little asterisk next to Atherton's score was joy and hope to this young innocent. He was the embodiment of St Paul's stirring cry to the Ephesians, to "stand your ground and after you have done everything to stand".

Whatever we had expected of the clean-cut, over-educated ingénu – Brearley's psychology, Hobbs's batting, Mrs Beeton's manners – it was not this, not the gritty endurances at the crease, not the stubble which like his stumps was most strongly rooted in times of greatest peril and certainly not that ruddy dirt, the stuff in his pockets that transformed him overnight from tousle-haired cherub to bounder. A friend recalls how I sat in the Lord's grandstand on the day of pocketgate, proclaiming loudly that Athers, my heroic, honourable Athers, could not possibly have done wrong. It turned out this was not strictly true but my trouser-defence remains watertight.

Yes, Athers' intransigence made him unpopular but I suspect that was part of the point, with the media at least. And no, uprooting Graeme Hick from the crease on 98 in the 1994–95 Sydney Test was not his finest hour. For many it confirmed he was not a 'people person'. Yet for almost a decade he negotiated what must have been a difficult relationship with Alec Stewart – an awkward ghost of the era of the amateur and the professional – into a mighty opening partnership. He brought us Angus Fraser's best years, coaxed the odd brilliant performance and, rarer, catch out of Phil Tufnell. He accommodated and utilised Darren Gough's ego to fuel morale. And he survived – sometimes thrived – under the autocratic regime of Ray Illingworth, which would have suffocated or crushed many.

He never gave the impression of having regrets

And boy, did he care. He was so committed to achieving his best that he repeatedly outplayed the rest of his side, some of it blessed with greater natural talent, with a bad back – an inherited rheumatic disease, ankylosing spondylitis, that caused him continual pain. The video of his 185 not out against South Africa at Port Elizabeth sits with *Citizen Kane* and *Gone With the Wind* in a grouping of worthy, laborious efforts, probably not to be watched again but triumphant vindication of all we knew and admired of the man. He could not turn his team into a bunch of winners but he could carry it.

In Atherton's media career he has been notable not only for the quality and fairness of his analysis and the lack of rancour but because, unlike many players-turned-pundits, he rarely makes comparisons with 'his day'. He would not want an apologia from me or anyone for the failings of his captaincy and would be the last to blame chop-'n'-change selection, the often one-dimensional nature of the bowling at his disposal or the frustratingly mercurial talents of his front-line batsmen.

Atherton has perfectionist tendencies but he never gave the impression of having regrets. I suspect, if he looks back, he wonders not if he did right by the team but if he did right by choosing a career in cricket when he was capable of pretty much anything. To that, I say: yes, Athers, you did.

EMMA JOHN is a former deputy editor of *The Wisden Cricketer* and *Observer Sport Monthly*

Toughing it out: Atherton floored trying to avoid a Courtney Walsh bouncer, Jamaica 1993–94

KEN BARRINGTON
by CHRISTOPHER MARTIN-JENKINS

Colonel Ken

**Ken Barrington brought stick-at-your-post dedication to Surrey and England.
A young Christopher Martin-Jenkins admired his guts – and his batting gloves**

I have an advantage, or perhaps it is a disadvantage, over at least some of the others writing about their cricketing heroes in this series. Most of us never get to meet our schoolboy paragons, let alone get to know them well.

It was different for me: I know and like Tom Graveney very much; I knew David Sheppard, Colin Cowdrey and Peter May equally well; Robin Marlar, Fred Trueman and Trevor Bailey became working companions; I have played golf with Ken Suttle, John Snow, Peter Parfitt and Peter Richardson; and either cricket or golf with players of more recent vintage like Dennis Amiss, or Derek Randall who, unless you are Australian, must be one of the most loveable cricketers ever.

But my choice falls on another of the same breed as Randall, another man who was always smiling and loved by everyone except Australians, Ken Barrington. Actually they remember him fondly now and admired him when he was frustrating them, much as Englishmen respected the likes of Bill Woodfull, Bill Lawry, Allan Border or Steve Waugh, because cussedness is a quality much appreciated in a Test cricketer by friends and foes alike.

> He was the craggy-faced,
> crinkly-haired son of a soldier.
> And proud of it

Barrington, the broad-batted defender of faltering causes, was a living paradox. A light-hearted joker for much of the time when he was not padded up, he worried for England as well as batting for them like Henry V at Agincourt. An excess of profound anxiety, and perhaps too many cigarettes, probably led to his early death. He began his cricket life as a carefree, attacking batsman but established himself as an ultra-reliable sticker, albeit one who occasionally reached Test hundreds with a six.

I first saw Ken batting for Surrey at The Oval, little imagining that I would one day bat and bowl with him in the nets there (for about a week, in fact, at pre-season nets, before the coach Arthur McIntyre realised that I lacked the necessary hardness to become a professional). Ken was a Test star then but some 10 years earlier he had made his way from Reading into the powerful Surrey XI and I was a schoolboy watching his late cut scudding across the turf to the point where I watched with my younger brother in the seats immediately behind the picket fence. "All the way, all the way," said a cloth-capped old boy next to us.

He played a big innings that day and I coveted his batting gloves: the new, white sausage-type that superseded the old green rubber JL Bryan Grasshoppers I used at school. His bat, of course, was a Stuart Surridge. I was at school in Eastbourne at the time but at home in the holidays just over the Sussex border into west Surrey, it was a dilemma whether the bat I longed for at Christmas should be a Gray-Nicolls 'Crusader' or an SS 'Perfect'.

In the intervening years I continued to admire from afar. Dropped after his first two Tests against South Africa in 1955, he was a tighter and more disciplined batsman by the time he got his place back four years later. He had learned thoroughly the professional batsman's first and second essentials: how to defend the castle and how to build an innings. Both were in keeping with his looks and his background: the craggy-faced, crinkly-haired son of a regular soldier in the British Army. And proud of it.

Once he had settled at the crease – booked in for bed and breakfast as he liked to say – he was as attractive a batsman even as some of the glorious stroke-players around him: May, Cowdrey, Graveney and Dexter. A little smaller than those four, he timed the ball with no less finesse, and he never lacked power. After 82 Tests, despite a late decline when his nerve began to fail a little in those pre-helmet days against short-pitched bombardments from the big West Indian fast bowlers, his average of 58 was better than any of them.

He was funny and a good mimic though his public-speaking was not so fluent

Chiefly this was because of his prolific form abroad. Once with England, with no other distractions such as the garage he ran at Bookham with his wife Ann, he would build his form from the start of the tour, to the extent where he could absolutely be depended upon to come good in the big games. He scored 1,329 runs at just on 70 in India and Pakistan in 1961–62; 1,763 at 80 in Australia and New Zealand the following winter and 1,128 at 86 in South Africa in 1964–65.

It was only in the third phase of his service to England that I got to know him well, when he managed the MCC tour of India, Sri Lanka and Australia in 1976–77. Media demands were fewer then but Ken's co-operation, trust and willingness to please combined to make my life as the BBC correspondent so much easier.

He was funny too. He was a good mimic, specialising in Alf Gover. When it came to public-speaking Ken was not so fluent. Asked by the Minister of Sport in Sri Lanka, during a long-winded speech, if the team had been in any way let down on the tour, he began his impromptu reply: "The first thing I'd like to say, Mr Minister, is that you 'aven't fallen down on any failings."

The Colonel, as by then he had come to be known by the players, had no obvious failings himself and his fatal heart attack in Barbados in 1981 at the age of 51 cast just the kind of worldwide pall over cricket that Bob Woolmer's death did earlier this year.

CHRISTOPHER MARTIN-JENKINS is the former chief cricket correspondent of *The Times* and a BBC *Test Match Special* commentator

BISHAN BEDI
by SURESH MENON

Graceful and gracious

**Watching a Bishan Bedi delivery was like
following the arc of a rainbow – only better**

Some years ago, while recuperating after surgery, I had a chance to put to the test HG Wells's dictum that the mind is the natural habitat of man. I was in intensive care and there were no books or television. To relax I had to travel inwards. And the image that helped was the poetry of Bishan Bedi's bowling. I could see in my mind's eye the easy run-up, the fluid action, the follow-through and the half-jump that confirmed to the batsman that he had been done. I marvelled at the contrast between the gentle curve of the ball in the air and its vicious pace off the wicket. The rainbow makes a beautiful arc but it is predictable. Bedi's arc was pleasing, and as a bonus its effect was unpredictable.

Bedi, the only Indian with over 1,500 first-class wickets, took 266 of them in his 67 Tests. It is necessary to descend to figures when discussing an artiste like Bedi only because, in sport, beauty without cruelty is a silly notion favoured by those long in tooth and short in memory. Every generation produces a great player who does not please the eye (Allan Border is a good example) but there is no great player who does not have the figures to show for it.

> ## Bedi believes
> ## in the brotherhood
> ## of spinners

I once saw Bedi leave a batsman stranded down the wicket when the ball went the wrong way after it had seemed set to come in with the arm. Bedi was 53 years old then and made no secret of his enjoyment at having fooled the batsman. This enjoyment was a big part of his game. "I dismissed Ian Chappell on 99 in a Test with just such a delivery," he recalled, demonstrating how he had held the ball in his palm and slid his wrist under it.

Bedi had the full repertoire of the finger-spinner and must rate as one of the two or three finest bowlers of his type the game has seen. Like Wilfred Rhodes, he "dismissed the batsman even before the ball had pitched" (Cardus's words), thanks to the ability apparently to yank it back at the last moment. Unlike Hedley Verity

and Derek Underwood, who both bowled much faster, Bedi didn't rely on the pitch for his wickets. He was the most generous of bowlers and wore his stature lightly.

This generosity extended to the opposition too. Bedi believes in the brotherhood of spinners, and all of them have access to his experience and wisdom. All they have to do is ask. On a Bangalore turner in 1986–87 a low-scoring match ended in Pakistan's favour by 16 runs after their left-arm spinner, Iqbal Qasim, was handed this gem from a now-retired Bedi: "On a turner the most dangerous ball is the one that goes through straight."

Against Tony Lewis's England in 1972–73 Bedi took 25 wickets to Bhagwat Chandrasekhar's 35, as the spinners harassed the batsmen. Bedi was often brought on in the third over, and had the batsmen in trouble from the start. It was a measure of both his confidence and his generosity that he found time to bowl to Dennis Amiss in the nets to help him sort out his problems.

You have to go back eight decades, to the Australian leggie Arthur Mailey, to find a kindred soul. Mailey took flak for helping out opponents. Extravagantly talented, both he and Bedi bowled with the lavishness of millionaires. Bedi's credo was first spelt out by Mailey, who said, "I'd rather spin it and see the ball hit for four than bowl a batsman out by a straight one." On another occasion Mailey said: "If I ever bowl a maiden over, it's not my fault but the batsman's." It is a sentiment Bedi would understand. Despite one-day cricket, he refused to bring his art down from the classical heights into the sphere of everyday utility. This refusal to compromise has been the hallmark of Bedi the player, the man, the administrator, coach and columnist.

Most people are publicly modest but privately quite immodest about their achievements. In Bedi's case it is the reverse. In a recent letter to me he wrote: "How I played my first Test is still an unsolved mystery. That I went on to captain the country is even more mind-boggling. Cricket is a funny game – always throwing up surprise packets." Few graceful performers are that gracious.

SURESH MENON is a Bangalore-based writer and a former editor of the *Indian Express* newspaper

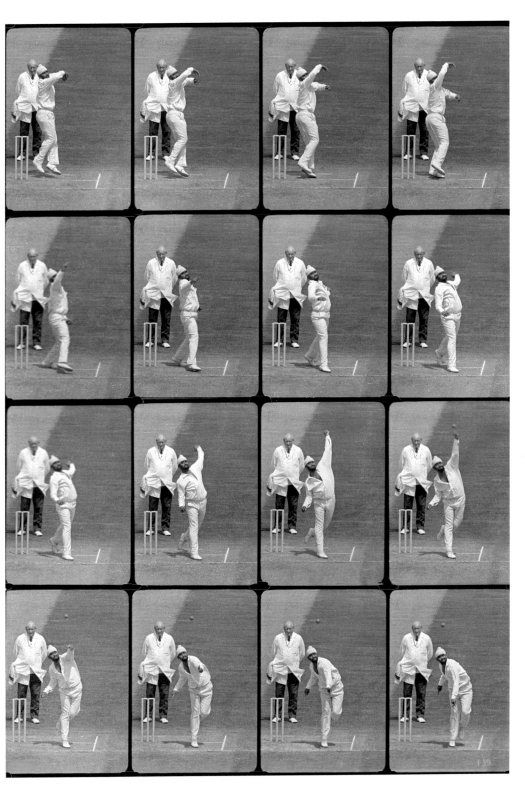

ALLAN BORDER
by MALCOLM KNOX

The artful stodger

In a team of strugglers and second-stringers, one man stood tall and unsmiling against the tide. Malcolm Knox worships Allan Border

When he was playing, Allan Border was never my favourite cricketer. I couldn't see past the glittering surfaces of Dennis Lillee, Doug Walters and Ian Chappell; then Vivian Richards, Clive Lloyd, and Michael Holding. Experience didn't add depth to my vision. In recent years my favourites have been dashers like Adam Gilchrist, princes of the willow like VVS Laxman, or fearsome athletes like Curtly Ambrose.

But just recently I went back to look at the Australian Team of the Century, voted in 2000. Every player in the XI was part of a golden age – from the years before the first World War, or playing around Don Bradman in the 1930s and 1940s, or around Chappell in the 1970s, or around Shane Warne and the Waughs in the last decade.

The 12th man in that side played in no great teams. He came into Australian cricket during World Series Cricket. He survived the reunification in 1979 and was building his name as a batsman when Australian cricket disintegrated in 1984. The team were being smashed. Kim Hughes relinquished the captaincy in tears then fled with a Test squad's worth of players to South Africa.

> ## I feel that Border's legacy will grow and grow over the years

What did Allan Border do? He had been to the Caribbean and played in Trinidad two of the greatest innings by any Australian anywhere: 98 not out and 100 not out, to earn the most miraculous draw. He'd proved himself as the one man who could stand up to them. So he took the captaincy, and in the next few years stood as the single pillar around which Australian cricket was rebuilt. He scored 11,174 Test runs, which no Australian has yet passed. He averaged over 50! He was the only one to make it into that Team of the Century who had spent most of his career surrounded by strugglers.

Also recently, I watched a TV documentary about Australian cricket in the 1980s.

Usually any sporting footage more than 10 years old looks inferior. Tennis players dab and slice, footballers walk around the park leisurely, cricket's bowlers look round-arm, and the batsmen – even Bradman – have distinctly dodgy techniques. Everything is slower. If you transplanted any player from the past into the present, they simply couldn't take the speed.

Yet when I watched those West Indian batteries – Holding, Malcolm Marshall, Joel Garner, Courtney Walsh, Ambrose – I saw attacks that were faster, nastier, and harder than today's. Pitches were most certainly quicker and bouncier. If you threw a 2006 vintage Ricky Ponting or Mohammad Yousuf or Sachin Tendulkar into a 1984 Test match against those West Indians in, say, Brisbane or Barbados, it's the present stars who would suffer.

So my appreciation of Allan Border has increased over time. As it should. I feel that Border's legacy will grow and grow over the years, as will Brian Lara's for similar reasons. Yet while Border developed, under duress, personal leadership skills, which Lara never has, he was never as glamorous as the man who took his world record.

Border stood in a baseballer's crouch, bat raised, ready to hop backwards and pull or cut the short ball. The Trinidad innings of 1983–84 were full of twitching jabs at balls aimed into his armpits. As he aged, he became a plainly unattractive batsman to watch, all punch, no grace.

He sprang to his feet and hurled his ball into the floor

But this is to forget what a wonderful attacker he was. He was arguably the best player of spin Australia has produced in 50 years. He scored 150 in each innings in a Test at Lahore in 1979–80 against Iqbal Qasim and Tauseef Ahmed. It would have been a dream to see him play Shane Warne.

Though his reputation is built on stodge and defiance, Border was also the finest all-round one-day cricketer of his time, alongside Viv Richards. I was at the SCG in 1984–85 when Border smashed an attack of Holding, Garner, Marshall, Winston Davis and Richards for 127 not out off 140 balls. He was also a brilliant fielder. In his early years he was a wonderful catcher in the hardest position, the wide third-to-fifth slips. His left-arm spinners were always useful, and in typical Border fashion, he under-used himself. In 1988–89 he took 11 wickets in a Test match against West Indies.

Yet the enduring image of Border is from off the field, from the decisive Adelaide Test of the 1992–93 series. Sitting in the dressing room, he clutched a lucky cricket ball in his hands. Finally we were going to beat them. Finally Border was going to beat them. Two runs short, Walsh got Craig McDermott with a lifter. The keeper caught the ball but the cameras caught Border. He sprang to his feet and hurled his ball into the floor. An entire career's worth of frustration captured in a single gesture.

Border retired one year before Australia won back the Frank Worrell Trophy. He never held it. But that's the way life is. It's not a fairytale. And Allan Border was never the fairytale hero. If I'm appreciating him more now, I'm glad. It shows some wisdom is finally getting through.

MALCOLM KNOX is a former chief cricket correspondent and literary editor of the *Sydney Morning Herald* and is the author of six books

GEOFF BOYCOTT
by SIMON WILDE

The broadacres' broadest bat

Simon Wilde is Geoff Boycott's No. 2 fan – you can guess who's No. 1

This is going to be hard to justify, I know. Press-box colleagues will now look the other way when they see me coming; certain former players will shake their heads reprovingly. "Doesn't he know what Boycott was like?" they'll be saying to themselves. "How blind he must have been . . ."

Well, yes, I do know what Boycott was like. Now. He had a reputation for thinking first of No. 1. But he was not alone in that. Cricket has seen many selfish players; some were just canny at hiding it. But back in the early 1970s, when I was growing up in Leeds, Boycott was a god. It is no use pretending otherwise. I was not alone in worshipping him. We all did – at least those of us who were not privy to the murderous undercurrents ripping through the Yorkshire dressing room as a once great club slid into mediocrity.

In truth the Yorkshire dressing room had never been a nice place – always hostile to newcomers and anyone who did not conform with the hard-nosed ethos that had won countless Championships. University graduates were viewed as mentally over-dressed for the simple task of winning matches by Grinding The Bastards Down. Boycott, not a university man but, almost as bad, a teetotaller, was regarded as a freak. He found himself isolated long before he had worked out he was head and shoulders above the rest as a batsman.

All that counted was the scorecard in the paper

Worshippers like me were part of the problem. The Yorkshire public had very high sporting standards. Most had grown up with the county routinely challenging for the Championship. Leeds United were among the best football teams in Europe. But in cricket things were changing fast. In an attempt to enliven county games it was made easier to sign overseas players. At a stroke this transformed the landscape.

With typical arrogance Yorkshire thought they could get along without foreigners – they were still selecting only players born in the county – and they soon became

a marginal force. In 1973 they even lost to Durham's amateurs. There were a few fine players – John Hampshire and Chris Old – but overall they were a grey team playing grey cricket in a small-minded cause.

That is except for Boycott. There could be no disputing his technical excellence. He could lay claim to being the best batsman in the world and was not only Yorkshire's mainstay but England's; his batting in Australia in 1970–71 had been central to winning back the Ashes. This was the sort of sporting excellence we Yorkies were used to.

OK, so we did not know much about his reputation for awkwardness with teammates. But when you are just entering your teens, it does not matter. All that counted was the scorecard in the paper . . . and there was Boycott, every day it seemed, top-scoring in another abject team performance. Amid such mediocrity the heroism seemed all the greater.

I was not alone. Hundreds in the county came to worship Boycott ahead of the team and, as has been seen with Brian Lara in the West Indies, the cult of personality usually leads to trouble. So, when Yorkshire removed Boycott as captain and later tried to remove him as player, public revolts were inevitable. Many felt that, whatever the problems, they simply could not be Boycott's fault. Briefly, and damagingly, his supporters took over the club and won him three more years as a player.

"I don't know why I'm shaking your hand, son, you never write anything nice about me."

Already Boycott's withdrawal from Test cricket between 1974 and 1977 had stretched my loyalty almost to breaking point. But, if it was stressful for me, it was not all plain sailing for him either. I see parallels between the problems he experienced as one of the first sports stars of the television age and those of George Best, also born in the 1940s. Although their reactions to dilemmas were different, they were both self-absorbed and confused young men, untrained to cope with a fierce public spotlight. Neither they, nor society, seemed to know how to handle the relationship.

For someone so easily painted black or white, Boycott's behaviour was rarely predictable. He was accused of opting out of Test cricket for his own ends but then showed loyalty to his country during the Packer affair and as a member of Mike Brearley's winning side became a revered and much more relaxed figure.

It was around this time that we first met. It was at an auction of sporting memorabilia in London, sent there for *Wisden Cricket Monthly*. The editor David Frith introduced me to Boycott, who shook my hand and said: "I don't know why I'm shaking your hand, son, because you never write anything nice about me." This was unwarranted; I had never written a hostile word about him.

But over time he redeemed himself. Around the press box he has always been happy to engage in cricket talk. The ultra-professionalism once applied to his batting is now applied to commentary. His illness, of course, mellowed him.

One encounter I will always remember. It was during the Centurion Test in January 2005, when on the back of Matthew Hoggard's match-winning effort at the Wanderers I had been asked to compile a list of the 10 greatest Yorkshire cricketers to play for England.

I spoke about it to Boycott and Darren Gough, both in my 10. While Gough was desperate to know where I had placed him – and was most upset to learn he was No. 8, below Ray Illingworth – Boycott did not once try to lobby himself up from No. 4, below Len Hutton, Fred Trueman and Herbert Sutcliffe. How is that for unselfish?

SIMON WILDE is cricket correspondent of the *Sunday Times* and the author of a number of books on cricket

ALLY BROWN
by HUGH MASSINGBERD

St John the Divine loses out

Hugh Massingberd swapped the church for The Oval and still found The Lord

The Lord has been my saviour but not quite in the sense that EW Swanton, my boss at *Barclays World of Cricket*, had in mind. In lowish water in the late 1970s I took refuge in Kennington, where Swanny urged me to seek salvation at St John the Divine. Unfortunately the church was so close to The Oval that I never made it to matins at St John's.

The ground had been a favourite of our family since my mother's first husband, Roger Winlaw, a Cambridge Blue later killed in the war, had been capped by Surrey in the 1930s. Fifty years on The Oval was not a particularly cheerful place, though the Caribbean spirit of Monte Lynch lit up the surly atmosphere, and from Surrey's youth system there was already talk of a tousle-headed youngster called Alistair Brown, an explosive batsman and off-break bowler who, as a 16-year-old schoolboy for Caterham, had won the 1986 Wetherall Award for the leading allrounder in English schools cricket.

In 1990 Ally Brown joined the Surrey staff at The Oval, where he was soon nick-named 'The Lord', or 'Lordy', as he supposedly batted like one. For me, steeped in romantic fantasies about the Golden Age when aristocratic amateurs flayed the crimson rambler to all parts, this was an irresistible recommendation.

The Lord certainly lived up to his name when he made his first-class debut in 1992. He rattled off three centuries in 79, 71 and 78 balls respectively, as well as the first of his 18 one-day hundreds. What has always thrilled me about him is his fine contempt for the so-called fear of failure; and the amazing thing is he still seems to bat in the same ultra-aggressive, supremely entertaining way in his mid-30s as he did in his early 20s.

From the moment he comes in he appears set on all-out attack. He is constantly looking for ways to score runs, ever searching for gaps and unexpected angles. His hand-eye co-ordination is astonishing, his bat-speed phenomenal. For a figure of such slight physique – he looks shorter than his 5ft 10in – he hits the ball incredibly hard and far. I still dream of his mighty blow at Lord's into the St John's Wood Road last summer.

The early part of a Brown innings can be an anxious time for nervous fans. In my usual vantage point near the Surrey changing room in the Bedser Stand I must resemble a contortionist as I writhe in my seat crossing fingers, thumbs and legs as

I pray that my hero will survive another ball. This is the price, I tell myself, that we must pay for genius. And, by God, it's worth it. For when The Lord gets in you can sit back and bask in his glory – the imperious off drives, the towering pulls and hooks, the straight sixes and crunching cuts.

Brown's conversion rate of half-centuries into hundreds is exceptional (in his first-class career he has scored 44 hundreds and 57 fifties). As a rule I am opposed to citing statistics to make a case but, paradoxically, they can be a useful weapon in fighting the prejudice of the bores who like to believe 'flashy dashers' are too inconsistent.

Brown's stats confound the canard that he is "unreliable". In first-class cricket he has scored 14,428 runs at an average of 44 (yet, disgracefully, he has never been selected for a Test); in one-day cricket it is 10,287 runs, averaging almost 32. He played 16 one-day internationals for England without being given a decent run in the side, despite scoring 118 against India and the fastest-ever fifty in the Texaco Trophy. His strike-rate in the Twenty20 is 162.

Over the last 15 years I have tried to plan my visits to The Oval around The Lord's manifestations at the wicket. Once, though only eight minutes from the ground, I found myself so transfixed by his lightning scoring rate on Ceefax that I failed to leave my chambers. Unfortunately I missed his 203 in a Sunday League game at Guildford (still the only double-century in the competition) and his 295 not out against Leicestershire (the highest ever score in Rutland) but I am eternally grateful that I was at The Oval on Wednesday June 19, 2002 – the best day of my life.

What Brown achieved that day has received nothing like the attention it deserves. With his 268 (160 balls, 12 sixes, 30 fours) against Glamorgan in a C&G match he did not just break but smashed to smithereens the world-record one-day score, Graeme Pollock's 222 not out in 1974–75 off 60 overs. And Brown's was off 50, the previous best for that being Sajid Ali's 197 not out in 1996–97.

As Trevor Jones, the Surrey librarian (whose book *268* is a splendid chronicle of that magical match), put it to me, it was like a sprinter knocking a second off the 100 metres record. No one has got within 61 runs of it since. During Brown's innings I was transported to nirvana. More prosaically the next day I sent him a cheque for £268 for his benefit fund and received a courteous acknowledgement.

I have never met my idol, though I think I got a touch at a slightly embarrassing glad-handing ceremony at The Oval to celebrate one of the three Surrey Championships in which Brown played such a vital role. For my part, since being diagnosed with advanced cancer, I have relied more than ever on this marvellous modern Master to cheer me up – and he has not let me down. I am now just living in hope of one more season of The Lord.

HUGH MASSINGBERD was the acclaimed obituaries editor of the *Daily Telegraph* from 1986 to 1994. He died in 2007

BRIAN CLOSE
by VIC MARKS

Learning at Close quarters

**He did not always remember Vic Marks' name but that did not stop
Brian Close earning a lasting place in the Somerset spinner's affections**

Two of my favourite cricketers have passed away this spring: Tom Cartwright and Arthur Milton, supreme craftsmen and supreme gentlemen, who played in an era when you could be a great cricketer without playing much for England.

Both were brave enough to try to coach me in my youth without the benefit of the ECB's Level 4 coaching certificate. They were the most influential coaches I came across – even though Arthur would only venture an opinion if you really pressed him; Tom was a little less reticent.

Both were very familiar with my favourite surviving cricketer, DB Close. In the 1950s Arthur briefly zipped down the wing for Arsenal and crossed the ball towards the Close forehead. Arthur used to delight in telling us how Close kept missing chances with headers because the ball was forever going over the bar. In training at Highbury they kept cajoling him to head the ball down, a skill he practised assiduously all of one week. Saturday came and Arthur crossed; Close soared, headed the ball down as prescribed with surprising power – it hit the turf and bounced over the bar.

As ever Closey had done everything perfectly and yet was still denied the success he deserved. In his darker moments, and I hope there haven't been too many of those, he reckoned that this was the story of his life.

> ## Close wasn't arrogant but
> ## I've never encountered a man with
> ## such a deep reservoir of self-confidence

Close was my first county captain. He had an immediate impact upon me; it took a little longer for me to impact upon him. For a while I might be addressed as "Pete lad" (Roebuck), "Phil lad" (Slocombe) or just occasionally "Vic lad", though never "Ian lad" – even Closey spotted the difference there.

He once asked me to sandpaper his bat as part of my 12th man duties (there were others: making him endless pots of tea and popping down to the bookies). Close's bat was one of many Stuart Surridges in our dressing room. I completed the task lovingly, leaving only the "DB" carefully inked on the shoulder. Close was unimpressed. It was Dennis Breakwell's bat.

We lost him for a while in 1976. At the age of 45, 27 years after his Test debut, he was chosen for three Tests against the ferocious pace attack of the West Indies. This, we learnt, was the first year in over two decades that Close had failed to put the Test match dates in his diary. He performed heroically against Andy Roberts, Michael Holding, Wayne Daniel and was upset to be dropped. He suspected that Tony Greig left him out since he was worried that he might be superseded as captain – by Close, of course. "Players kept looking at me when I was at short leg, so I put 'em in right place," he would tell us upon his return from the Tests.

In his last – and 22nd – Test he was battered at Old Trafford on an uneven pitch against West Indian pacemen in the most ruthless frame of mind, disinclined to grovel. He returned immediately to the Somerset side for a Gillette Cup match at Edgbaston. A fiery young Bob Willis hit him in the chest; his legs buckled like a beleaguered boxer's and he hit the floor. He got up to top score in the Somerset innings.

Ray Illingworth once told me that Close was a bit of a hypochondriac in his youth, always off the field for something – until they made him captain at Yorkshire. By the time I came across him stories of his bravery were legendary; they were also true.

Close was never arrogant, but I've never encountered a man with such a deep reservoir of self-confidence. He was never out through his own fault. It might be because the 12th man had brought the wrong-flavoured chewing gum or poor advice from the preceding batsman. "You told me it was swinging; you didn't tell me it was seaming as well," he once chastised a colleague after becoming the third victim of a hat-trick at Trent Bridge.

"I can play him all right – but you might struggle," he told Peter Roebuck

Unlike Cartwright, with whom he combined to turn Somerset into a good team, he was not a natural coach, even though he had an instinctive feel of how to win cricket matches. Peter Roebuck, in one of his first games for the county, once wandered down the pitch to Close between overs in search of some guidance. "I can play him all right – but you might struggle" was not quite what Peter was looking for.

Of course Close was a remarkable, intuitive captain, who led England seven times, winning six matches and drawing one. England won his first Test in charge in 1966 at The Oval when he memorably caught Garry Sobers first ball at short leg after a plan, hatched with John Snow, had come to fruition. A long England career beckoned again but somehow it all went wrong.

A few years later Sobers came out to bat for Nottinghamshire at Taunton when

Hard man: Close aged 45, is hit by a bouncer at Old Trafford, England v West Indies, 1976

Close was captaining Somerset. Close had been fielding at short leg, of course, and Cartwright was bowling. Between them in their contrasting ways they knew all there was to know about the game.

The crowd shuffled to the edge of their seats. The world's greatest allrounder pitched against the ultimate English medium-pacer and this inspirational, unconventional leader. Here was a moment to savour. They watched Close move slowly towards the end of Cartwright's run-up as Sobers took guard. An important conversation was about to take place. What cunning plan would be hatched, what unorthodox field placement? What would Close's fertile brain come up with this time? "Right, Tom lad," said Close. "This lad's a left-hander." Whereupon he turned and walked all the way back to his post, perilously close to Sobers, at forward short leg.

VIC MARKS, who played for Somerset and England, is cricket correspondent of *The Observer* and a summariser for BBC Radio's *Test Match Special*

JOHN DYE
by SIMON O'HAGAN

To Dye for

Some players are generous on the pitch. Some are generous off it.
Some are both, which is why **Simon O'Hagan** will always love John Dye

Lord's on the morning of September 4, 1971. My team, Kent, are taking on Lancashire in the Gillette Cup final. It's a clash of the heavyweights, and the ground is already buzzing.

Lancashire, fresh from an epic semi-final victory against Gloucestershire, are reckoned to be the best one-day team in the land. They boast the great West Indian Clive Lloyd and leading Englishmen in David Lloyd, Barry Wood, and Peter Lever. But we've got our own big names – Asif Iqbal, Mike Denness, Brian Luckhurst, Alan Knott, Derek Underwood. We definitely fancy our chances.

I'd like to be able to say I was there. Instead, I was on holiday in Cornwall, aged 13, watching on a fuzzy black-and-white TV. As the players took the field, there was one in particular I was looking out for. He wasn't a star. In fact, I feared he might not even be picked.

John Dye was a burly, left-arm quick bowler who did his stuff for Kent without fuss or fanfare. He had grown up in the Medway towns, only a few miles from where I lived. He had the physique of a prop forward but none of the stolidity. With his rolling gait as he approached the wicket, power seemed to accumulate with every stride. He was a tremendous sight. He would arch his back, plant his foot, and whip his arm through. There was a hint of a swagger.

But what really mattered to me about Dye was that he had taught me how to bowl properly. As a cricket-mad youngster, I spent my winters in the indoor nets in Chatham where Dye occupied himself between seasons. Most first-class players you grew up admiring from a distance. Here was one who had adjusted my position at the moment of delivery.

I'd also discovered what a great bloke he was – a man of the people who was good-humoured and generous and who betrayed no sense that this work was beneath him. He loved cricket, he loved to see it played the right way, and he loved to pass on his knowledge and enthusiasm.

So the player who got the nod for Kent that day – it was a close-run thing between him and the young allrounder Graham Johnson – wasn't just John Dye. He was my John Dye. And when Lancashire went out to bat, it was Dye who was given the first over. Come on, Dye! Up he stepped, and in he came, and his second ball was a beauty which had Wood lbw for nought. Yes!

As I recall, Dye was virtually unplayable that morning. He made the ball lift, he slanted it across, and he brought it back – the thing that all left-arm over bowlers are supposed to do, but rarely can. Bob Cottam, who played alongside Dye at Northamptonshire later in the 1970s, told me "he picked up so many lbws bowling to right-handers it was unbelievable."

Dye dismissed Harry Pilling for his second wicket, which was to be his last meaningful contribution to the match. But what a contribution it was. Clive Lloyd scored a brilliant 66 to help Lancashire to 224, and Kent's run chase ended when Jack Bond took a magnificent diving catch at extra cover to dismiss Asif.

As it turned out, that defeat was one of Dye's last matches for Kent. The county is notorious for discarding good players before their time and their treatment of Dye was typical. He could have taken stacks more wickets for Kent. Instead, he took them for Northamptonshire, where he was a key player in one of the most successful sides in the county's history.

Dye was well liked by team-mates, Cottam told me, but his career was far from all sweetness and light. You could sense the outsider in him. He had his pride. Matthew Engel, then covering Northants for the local paper, tells the story of how Dye once stopped him in his car. "He wanted me to know that the paper had got his batting average wrong. It wasn't 2.62 or something. It was 2.98. He was only half joking."

Dye's sacking by Kent rankled so badly that, according to Cottam, he couldn't bring himself to talk about his time there. He was equally unhappy when, in 1977, Northants let him go, even though he was 35. But the game was changing, and Dye was not exactly the most adaptable of cricketers. His attitude to batting and fielding was that of someone who didn't believe they were part of the job description. Dye was a traditionalist. You had your role and that was it. As Andrew Radd, a Dye fan and Northants-based cricket writer, told me: "All I can say is I'm glad John wasn't around when Twenty20 came in."

Radd grew up supporting Northants the way I had grown up supporting Kent. The memory of Dye that stands out for him almost mirrors my own. This time it's the 1976 Gillette Cup final. Again the opposition are Lancashire, again Dye opens the bowling, and again it's explosive. He bowls Farokh Engineer first ball. His match figures were 7-3-9-1.

For an unassuming man, Dye had an amazing relish for the big occasion. But the game meant everything to him at the opposite end of its spectrum, too. I like to think he discovered that when he was helping 12-year-olds like me back in 1970, because in retirement he took up as a schools coach proper, spending 20 years at Wellingborough. "He was brilliant," a colleague told me. "The boys loved him."

Dye, now 63, went with his wife to live in Spain a few years ago. I'd just like to say, "Gracias, John".

SIMON O'HAGAN is deputy comment editor and former cricket correspondent of the *Independent on Sunday*

Unplayable in the morning: Dye bowls for Kent in 1971

Delhi delight: Edmonds celebrates the dismissal of India's Anshuman Gaekwad in 1984–85

PHIL EDMONDS
by NICK GREENSLADE

From rucks to riches

The Middlesex and England spinner was a one-off, a rebel with a Rolls-Royce and a talent for making trouble and money that appealed to Nick Greenslade

The first time I heard Phil Edmonds speak he was, fittingly, talking about money. It was the high-water mark of Thatcherism in the late 1980s and he was asked about attitudes to wealth on either side of the Atlantic. "If someone in the United States sees a guy driving a Rolls-Royce, he'll say to himself, 'Good on him,'" Edmonds observed. "In Britain people just look on enviously and want to knock you."

Edmonds was not the first or last English plutocrat to make this unfavourable comparison but it was not the kind of comment one expected from an England cricketer. I had suspected there was something different about the Middlesex spinner since I first came across him in 1982. Recalled for England's home series against India after an exile of three years, he came with talk of "an unsettling influence".

The more I saw, the more intrigued I became. When he took the field it was with a Swatch on his wrist: alone among the England team Edmonds had negotiated a sponsorship deal with a watch brand. Asked to field around the bat, he would encroach ever closer, allowing his shadow to fall across the business part of the pitch. Invariably he had a choice word for the batsman. Chat, like wealth, was not something Edmonds lacked.

He was as comfortable in the boardroom as the dressing room

Yet he also had talent. On England debut, against Australia in 1975, he took 5 for 28 with his left-arm spinners. It was a remarkable introduction to Test cricket. His success stemmed from height and strength, which brought considerable turn and flight, as well as bounce. This last ingredient was apparent when he occasionally threw in a bouncer, upsetting his own unsuspecting keeper as much as the batsman.

Though never an allrounder, Edmonds was a useful lower-order bat. In that summer of 1982 he and Derek Randall – an odd couple, to be sure – rescued England from a middle-order collapse and set up a decisive win in the first Test. Edmonds hit 64.

A Test average of 17, however, indicates that he did not fulfil his potential. A blasé approach to dismissal did not help. As his county team-mate Simon Hughes has written, Edmonds would often walk back to the pavilion "chuckling with a mixture of mild disbelief and perverse pleasure". For captains this must have been infuriating. For me it completed the picture of a loveable maverick.

The son of a colonial property developer in northern Rhodesia, a Cambridge graduate and a man as comfortable in the boardroom as dressing room, he looked ideal establishment material. But he was much more a son of Africa than of Empire; he was involved in the black independence movement in the late 1960s.

The result of his idiosyncrasies was that he missed more Tests than he played

His anti-establishment credentials were confirmed by his continual disagreements with authority, particularly Mike Brearley. The England and Middlesex captain was the last person he should have been upsetting but Edmonds was his own man. After a spat too many he pinned Brearley to the wall and warned him to "lay off". Later I heard he had treated his biographer Simon Barnes in the same manner.

Despite their differences, Brearley, as fine a judge as any, rated Edmonds. In *The Art of Captaincy* he writes that he appreciated his spinner's shrewd cricketing brain. Brearley put him in the same awkward-but-intelligent category as Geoff Boycott and it is perhaps not surprising that this abrasive pair struck up a friendship. Boycott called them the 'Fitzwilliam twins' – Fitzwilliam being his home town in Yorkshire and Edmonds' Cambridge college.

Edmonds' cardinal sin, however, was to marry a woman of independent means and mind. During the 1980s England cricketers were not expected to bring their wives on tour, never mind have them write about the experience. Shortly after publishing *Another Bloody Tour*, her best-selling account of the disastrous trip to the Caribbean in 1985–86, Frances Edmonds was probably known to more people than her husband, a point not lost on Tim Zoehrer. "At least I have an identity," the Australian keeper said in response to the usual sledging. "You're only Frances Edmonds' husband."

The result of his idiosyncrasies was that he missed more Tests (75) than he played (51). His most successful period came when he played under a captain, David Gower, who was equally laid-back. On Gower's 1984–85 trip to India, the last England victory in that country, Edmonds and his fellow spinner Pat Pocock bowled long spells to tie up the batsmen. The following summer he was an integral member of the team that won back the Ashes from Allan Border's Australia, and he was no less important on the victorious trip to defend them in 1986–87.

After that, business began to get in the way of the day job and in 1987 ads retired from first-class cricket. However, another improbable comeback remained. In 1992, aged 41 and pepped up by an industrial supply of painkillers – there was talk of him being shielded from the drug testers – he defied his ailing back, arrived at Trent Bridge (in a Rolls-Royce, naturally) and took 4 for 48 for an injury-struck Middlesex.

Today he is chairman of the county but no less controversial. His recent business dealings in war-torn Sudan have raised eyebrows among the blazer brigade as his wining and dining of commercial associates during luncheon intervals once did. I do not suppose for a moment that he gave a damn and I would be disappointed if he did.

NICK GREENSLADE is deputy sports editor of the *Sunday Times* and a former deputy editor of *Observer Sport Monthly*

FAROKH ENGINEER
by MICHAEL HENDERSON

Done with a flourish

The batting was adventurous, the keeping extravagant, the smile ready. All in all the exotic charm of Farokh Engineer was too much for Michael Henderson

I first went to Old Trafford in 1967, the so-called Summer of Love. Lancashire were anything but a groovy side at the time, though the players looked pretty smart to my eight-year-old eyes, and it was not until Jack Bond took over the captaincy in 1968 that their cricket began to improve. That was Farokh Engineer's first year at the club and it did not take him long to become my hero.

Engineer had caught my attention the previous summer when he kept wicket for India on their tour. There was something exotic about the way he walked to the crease – it was a proper mincing walk – and his flourishes behind the stumps were also eye-catching. He was a show-off. And though he frequently got out when he appeared well set, there was something appealing about his batting. There was a hint of danger and, remember, in 1967, when Geoff Boycott was dropped by England for slow scoring after making a double-century at Headingley, there was some pretty dull cricket. Looking back from this vantage point, when young folk are introduced to cricket through the frenzied Twenty20 game, it is puzzling to see how strongly I fell for this time-consuming summer ritual.

> Very often I wanted
> to go home when
> he was out

With the mincing walk, his engaging manner (a smile was never far away), that wide stance and his eagerness to charge the bowlers, even the quick ones, it was not difficult to warm to Engineer. He radiated an enthusiasm for cricket that one did not sense in the personalities of, say, Ken Snellgrove and John Sullivan, admirable pros though they were. He was also Indian, a Parsee from Bombay, and that in itself was exotic. To this day I have always had a soft spot for Indian cricketers – most of them anyway.

Yet Engineer usually disappointed me. Whenever I saw him bat, the delight of anticipation soon turned to dust. Very often I wanted to go home when he was out,

With the bat: Engineer at the crease for India against England at The Oval in 1971

for the day had lost its bloom. As John Arlott noted, he had strokes that many heavier run-makers envied, but the long innings was beyond him. At school I picked up the papers every summer's day to see how he had got on and read with joy of his maiden century for Lancashire, against Glamorgan. But the joy was compounded by another feeling, disappointment, that I had not been there to see it.

Even when Clive Lloyd joined Lancashire in 1969 Engineer remained my favourite. Lancashire won the Sunday League that year, and again in 1970, when they also beat Sussex in the first of three successive Gillette Cup triumphs. Those really were the glory days. However much one-day cricket has changed in the last three decades, nothing and nobody will erase my memories of that Lancashire side, and Engineer's part in it.

The finest moment came not in one of those highly charged one-day games but in a Championship match at Buxton in July 1971. Lancashire lost five early wickets to Derbyshire, and Alan Ward was bowling very fast, but Engineer kept pulling him into the bushes at midwicket. He reached the century I had longed to see him make and had made 141 when he was finally out. That, at least as much as the famous Gillette semi-final against Gloucestershire later that month, is the abiding memory of 1971.

With the gloves: Engineer runs out England's John Jameson in 1971

My bias towards Engineer went beyond the bounds of blood. He had been dropped from the Rest of the World side that played England in five unofficial Tests in 1970, so when he was at the crease at The Oval the following summer, knocking off the runs to help India win their first series here, I was almost as pleased as the Indians who led an elephant on to the outfield to celebrate.

I can see now that he was not the best wicketkeeper in the world, as we liked to think at Old Trafford. Alan Knott was and Bob Taylor was magnificent. Nor was Engineer an outstanding batsman, though he was capable of the occasional bracing innings. Nor was he always a model of rectitude. At the time, though, any criticism of him was misplaced for, in my eyes, he could do no wrong.

The end came quickly. At the end of the 1976 season, two months after I had left school, and two weeks after Lancashire had lost a Gillette Cup final, he left the club. At the start of that season my other sporting hero, Francis Lee, the marvellous footballer for Manchester City, had also retired, so the summer of 1976 represented the end of childhood. It did not seem like that at the time. But when the 1977 season began there was a small hole in my life.

It is not always wise to meet heroes. I have met Engineer twice, inconsequentially, but that he played when he did, and in the manner that he did, will always be good enough for me. Whenever I remember those days I am nine again and the world seems full of possibilities. Arlott was right. He adorned the game more than players who ended their careers with better figures, and there is a lot to be said for being a pleasure-giver.

Those you warm to in the early days mean the most to you

Ian Botham was the greatest English player I saw and he too was a hero. The thing is, he was everybody's hero. Sobers, Kanhai, Viv, Majid Khan, Warne, Mark Waugh, Azharuddin, Dravid, Wasim Akram, Donald: they have all meant a lot to me. But those you warm to in the early days, who mould your imagination, mean the most to you, whether they were great or not. So I remain faithful to the memory of 'Rookie' and recall Fitzgerald's valediction to Jay Gatsby: "So we beat on, boats against the current, borne back ceaselessly into the past."

MICHAEL HENDERSON is a former cricket correspondent of the *Daily Telegraph* and writes on cricket and the arts for *The Times*, *The Wisden Cricketer* and *The Spectator*

ANGUS FRASER
by ANDREW MILLER

Parsimony not panache

In Angus Fraser Andrew Miller found a role model for the anti-athlete

The summer of 1989 was a desperate time for an impressionable 11-year-old to get hooked on cricket. Four thumping Test defeats, 29 players, a raft of rebel-tour defectors and Gooch lbw b Alderman 0. Try picking the positives out of that.

And yet, there was one. A lone pillar of rectitude in a ransacked temple. His shoulders were perpetually stooped but his spirit was never broken and, while the charlatans and showponies were being ruthlessly disembowelled by Allan Border's freakishly focused Australians, Angus Fraser just ran in and bowled, and ran in and bowled, and ran in and bowled.

I had hit upon my hero largely by accident. I had been struggling, as a patriotic Scotsman born in Germany and raised in Dorset, to justify on the one hand my loathing of the England rugby team and on the other my adoration of all things leather and willow. Fraser, born near Wigan and based in Middlesex but blatantly as Scottish as they came, was all the evidence an 11-year-old needed to have his cake and eat it.

But as soon as I saw him bowl, I realised the connection went deeper than any spurious claims to shared ancestry. In Fraser I recognised an anti-athlete at the peak of his powers, a sportsman to inspire the fat, the slow, the red-faced and the sweaty. I was all of these and more. I loved cricket but was exquisitely hopeless at it.

My mother spotted his loping frame in the distance and I was off, hurtling to intercept him

Fraser taught me there was another way. Line and length, rhythm and control. Parsimony over panache. Every spare moment was spent in the nets, lumbering in, reaching high, competing for the first time with my flash athletic peers who had all the pace but none of the guile. When I was picked as first-change for the junior 3rd XI, it was the proudest day of my life.

As the summer wore on and England's poundings continued to mount, Fraser's Pyrrhic successes became the only thing worth clinging to. Take the fifth Test at Trent

Bridge. I surveyed it from afar, having been whisked away on a family holiday to Yugoslavia, but a sneaky glimpse at a rare copy of the *Daily Mail* told me all I needed to know. Australia had amassed 602 for 6 declared but Fraser had put his peers to shame with 52.3 overs, 18 maidens, 2 for 108. It was genius repackaged as futility.

But then suddenly Fraser's wickets started coming as well and my hero worship went into overdrive. Five for 28 in 20 overs at Sabina Park, as West Indies were sensationally toppled on home turf; eight in the match against India at Lord's, when Gooch scored 333; and another five-for in the very next Test at Old Trafford. When my parents caught me bouncing on the sofa in glee after India had been skittled for 432 (Fraser 5 for 124), they realised it was time to bite the bullet and indulge my odd obsession.

And so off we went to The Oval to watch my very first Test. It was an abominable day's play dominated by a tedious Ravi Shastri century, but at the close, I finally met my man. In fact I almost missed him. I'd been immersed in autograph hunting behind the pavilion, ticking off the names like a trainee anorak but my mother spotted Fraser's loping figure plodding into the distance, and bang, I was off – hurtling down the Harleyford Road to intercept him as he fled. I don't recall speaking as I thrust my bat under his nose. Adrenalin could carry me only so far.

But no sooner had I met him, he was gone. A mystery hip condition, brought on by yet more Ashes futility, left his career hanging by a thread. For two seasons I searched for him in the county scorecards but under ARC Fraser I found only an imposter with a handful of expensive appearances to his name. "Why aren't you playing Angus? We need you," I shocked myself by shouting when I bumped into him again at The Oval in 1991. "I want to play," came the plaintive response.

But he couldn't, and didn't, and I had no choice but to move on. Mike Atherton became my new favourite player (no other bowler cut the mustard) and I took pleasure in England's rare moments of success. But I still checked the Middlesex card every week, hoping that the big man would return.

> I was smugly reminding everyone that
> Fraser was the greatest medium-fast
> bowler that ever walked the earth

And then suddenly it happened. A spell of 7 for 40 against Leicestershire in 1993 and the cry went up from the shires that Fraser had got his 'snap' back. Two games later he – and I – were back at The Oval for the sixth Test against Australia. But how would I respond? I was now 15 with my first vaguely teenage pretensions – clearly too grown-up for such childish obsessions. Like hell I was. Eight match-winning wickets later and I was smugly reminding anyone I'd ever met that Fraser was the greatest medium-fast seam bowler that had ever walked the earth.

And I was still doing it five years later as Fraser routed the West Indians in

Trinidad. Did he lose a certain something after his injury? Maybe. But in an era of slim pickings for players and fans alike he still cared more passionately than any other English bowler of his generation. His main failing was that he was a sweaty knacker who looked defeated after a single delivery. But, as the man himself has been known to grumble, "Bowling is bloody hard work." It was never in Fraser's nature to try and pretend otherwise.

ANDREW MILLER is the UK editor of Cricinfo.com and has modelled his bowling style on Angus Fraser

JOEL GARNER
by DEREK PRINGLE

Big bounce, big laughs, Big Bird

Derek Pringle remembers sharing a pitch – and a rum or three –
with a genial giant from Barbados

Envy is never a particularly productive emotion in sport unless you can do something about it. But try as I did during my own career to figure out ways to emulate my favourite cricketer, Joel Garner, I knew that short of being stretched on the rack such class was always likely to elude me.

Garner, or 'Big Bird' as he was known in cricket circles after the Doctor Bird (a Caribbean species distinguished by its stilt-like legs), was a giant fast bowler possessed of an unerring control of line, length and temperament. His pace was not express, at least not until late in his Test career when they wound him up and gave him the new ball, but he was quick enough to keep the ambition of most batsmen pegged back to somewhere between survival and singles.

Occasionally he would get collared, something Graham Gooch managed in a brilliant 122 for Essex against Somerset at Taunton in 1981. But such occurrences were rare. Bird had already scrambled my stumps in that match despite warnings from team-mates to "watch out for his yorker". What the clever-clogs never mentioned was the set-up that preceded it, where he pushed you ever further back with a series of jarring lifters before delivering – with a cunning extra yard of pace – that guillotine ball.

Actually his yorker was a sucker ball for scuppering the callow and the tailender and he rarely used it when trying to dismiss proper batsmen. Against them the game was to give away as few runs as possible, wear down any resistance with unwavering accuracy and pick up three or four wickets for spit. It wasn't a cunning plan but boy was it successful.

At 6ft 8in tall he was a fearsome sight and sound, his bellowed appeal in deep basso profundo making the air quiver with expectation. In nature, plenty of animals make themselves bigger or louder to frighten others but in general it is a bluff. With Bird there was no pretence and you got exactly what was threatened: quick and bouncy bowling that tested a batsman's mettle and technique to the max.

His Test record of 259 victims in 58 matches at an average of 20.97 does not look especially remarkable now that Shane Warne and Muttiah Muralitharan have broken the 700 barrier. But since Test pitches were first covered in the 1970s (a huge advantage for batsmen), only his fellow Bajan and West Indies team-mate, Malcolm Marshall, has a lower average (20.94) among those with over 100 wickets to their name.

"Watch out for his yorker": Pringle lbw b Garner 2, Lord's 1984

Bird never took 10 wickets in a Test but that was more to do with those around him than any failing on his part. For the first half of his Test career, from 1977 to 1982, he was part of the greatest pace quartet the world has ever seen. Sharing the stage with fast bowlers as deadly as Michael Holding, Andy Roberts and Colin Croft inevitably meant the spoils were shared around. In any case, his role – as the Lomotil that blocked up the scoring rate – rarely afforded him the luxury of mopping up the tail.

What set Bird apart from his peers, and remember this is when West Indies ruled the cricket world with a ruthless swagger, was his geniality. OK, he was programmed to kill when he had a ball in his hand but off the field I have never seen him wearing anything but a face-splitting grin.

Our friendship began 28 years ago when I was at Cambridge and I took him and a few of his Somerset team-mates to a party the night before we played them at Fenner's. Joel must have had a good time as he reminds me of it even now: "Man those student chicks were friendly."

Like many Bajans he is a devotedly social animal, liking nothing more than to regale friends with rum bottle in hand. We've had crazy nights out in Sydney, Brisbane, London and Bridgetown, the last all the more special for being his home turf. But you need a supple neck (at 6ft 5in even I have to look up to him) and real stamina, for it takes a long time for those long, hollow legs to fill.

Once in Barbados, he took me for lunch at a kiosk in Oistins, well away from the reddening tourists on the west coast. It was, he insisted, the best food on the island, the cooking done by the dinner lady from his old school. "I been eating this since I was six. How else you think I get this big," he chuckled as we tucked in to a delicious feast of chicken stew, callaloo and macaroni pie.

When you're as good as him there is no need to worry about the small details, something revealed by his master plan when captaining Barbados in 1986. "It's quite simple. Me and Macko [Marshall] open the bowling and nip out the top order. We have a rest and the other bowlers come on and keep it tight. Then me and Macko come on and blast out the tail. We have a bat, get a hundred lead and bowl them out again."

Barbados were the best club side there has ever been. They should have been sponsored by Carlsberg

Six years earlier, the Barbados attack had been even more fierce: Bird, Marshall, Sylvester Clarke and Wayne Daniel. With Gordon Greenidge and Desmond Haynes to open the batting it was probably the best club side there has ever been. They should have been sponsored by Carlsberg.

He's been retired 20 years now, a period in which West Indies cricket has slipped down the gurgler. Unlike many of his generation he is not bitter about the decline and has even tried to help. But that is Bird – great bowler but even greater human being.

DEREK PRINGLE played 30 Tests for England between 1982 and 1992. He is now cricket correspondent of the *Daily Telegraph*

ADAM GILCHRIST
by NICHOLAS SHAKESPEARE

Let the walking do the talking

Adam Gilchrist has teeth to die for and his batting wasn't bad either, says Nicholas Shakespeare

It is hard to be an English cricket fan in Tasmania. "We're going to murder you next year," was one of the milder sledgings I received in the corner store when I commiserated over Australia's Ashes defeat in 2005. And murder us they did. Still, as I struggle to teach my sons cricket on Nine Mile Beach, I nurture a fantasy that Max – aged 8, b. Wiltshire – will one day open the bowling for England against Benedict – aged 5, b. Hobart (in the same hospital as Tasmania's most famous son but unremarkable slip catcher, Errol Flynn).

Tasmania's influence on the cricket pitch has never looked firmer than since the retirement of David Boon, "the keg on legs". A Tasmanian, Ricky Ponting, captains Australia. A Tasmanian, tall and wiry Troy Cooley, one of the fastest bowlers the state has produced, coached England during that summer of 2005, exciting the local headline: "Losing the Ashes to England, it's just not cricket." And, helping to determine just what is cricket, is another Tasmanian, Keith Bradshaw, chief executive of MCC since 2006.

> ## Gilly changed
> ## the nature of
> ## Test cricket

I was ignorant of the game's influence on my own work until *The Wisden Cricketer's* deputy editor pointed out that a novel I had set in Tasmania, *Secrets of the Sea*, was wriggling with cricket references. (A country estate agent is known as "the David Boon of real estate"; the Australian heroine, concerned about her inability to have children, tells her husband, the son of English parents, that she is driving to Launceston for a test. "A Test? Are England playing?") Alerted, I flick through my latest novel to discover the central character "batting away" a difficult question. Moreover, whenever he thinks of God the image that floats to mind is of a tall man gesticulating from the boundary. The novel ends with hero and heroine walking out into the winter night "to face whatever the darkness was about to bowl at them".

Ton up: Gilchrist reaches 100 against England at Perth in 2006–07, off 57 balls, only one short of Viv Richards' Test record

It was my grandfather, the writer SPB Mais, who kindled this interest. He was a "duffer and rabbit of the first order" who, in a long village cricket career, never got called upon to bowl and was noted for dropping catches. But he risked prison – and even lost his family home near Brighton – in an ultimately successful battle with the local council for the right of Southwick Cricket Club to continue playing on the village green. And while he did not live to watch my favourite cricketer chip one of his gracefully timed boundaries, he would have applauded my choice and not given a brass razoo that I have chosen an Australian; he would, in fact, share the unmodish conviction that it is how you play the game that matters a lot more than who you play it for.

I was in Tasmania in November 2007 when Adam Gilchrist hit his 100th Test six at Hobart, slogging Muttiah Muralitharan out of the ground. The innings was typical of Gilly, a reminder of how he had changed the nature of Test cricket. A fast-hitting left-hander – like all the great batsmen – he legitimised its passing from a slow sport to a one-day speed. For 120 years it goes along at 2.5–3.5 runs an over. Then Gilchrist comes in and now 4.5 runs is considered quite attainable. On this November day he made an unbeaten 67. No one could have hit the ball more sweetly or in his own way. Few people have invented a shot; it's as rare as inventing a new knot for a tie. One thinks of Grace, Ranji's leg glance . . . and Gilchrist's signature chip over slips.

Also in Hobart three days earlier Gilchrist had won the player's poll for Australia's greatest one-day international player. His modest reaction was in keeping with what, for Gilchrist admirers, is saintly about him. Even his surname has Christ in it.

He did not come into the national team until quite late – waiting around for Ian Healy to leave. So he had catching up to do. But his furious pace was only part of it. There was, for instance, that cap, his ears peeking out from underneath. You never saw him without it. Nor did you hear him sledge. And he had such a healthy, clean-living face. "The excellent Western Australian teeth Martin Amis would give his left testicle for," as one friend put it.

Sometimes, one suspected, he walked even without being out

He's inventing shots; he's scoring faster; he's hitting harder than anyone else. And then, to top it all, he has to keep wicket to Shane Warne. He has to keep wicket to the best bowler who's ever been. But it's a double act. A bowler like that needs a keeper like that to keep him going.

He retired at the top of his game (timing again) the day after passing a record 416 Test dismissals. His batting average was in the high 40s and included the second fastest Test century. In an age of celebrity he was that, too, without wanting to be anything more than a sportsman.

And then there was his walking. Sometimes, one suspected, he walked even without being out. But if he stayed, you could be damn sure there was no doubt. In cricket the umpire's decision is right, even if he's wrong. What Gilchrist did, in the way cricket tends to throw up paradoxes, was to say: sometimes when the umpire's right, he's wrong.

As Max Davidson writes in his book on sportsmanship, *It's Not the Winning That Counts*: "Now that Gilchrist has retired, the honesty he epitomised remains the template by which other cricketers will be judged."

NICHOLAS SHAKESPEARE is a journalist and author. He is the author of the novel *Secrets of the Sea* and the travelogue *In Tasmania*

GRAHAM GOOCH
by PATRICK KIDD

King of the Colchester castle

**Patrick Kidd was born to worship Gooch – in the same hospital as the batsman,
who was making a ton at the time and was still making them 20 years later**

I saw Graham Gooch's bottom last year – not his real bottom but a good impersonation.
It was attached to Varun Chopra, the Essex and England Under-19 opening batsman
who has been coached by Gooch – and it shows.

The high lift of the bat, the backside thrust out towards square leg, the left elbow
high, the eyes staring straight down the barrel of his left shoulder – all Chopra needed
was a bushy moustache and the likeness would have been complete.

It took me back 15 or more summers to those golden days in 1990–92 when an
Essex man with a paunch and a weary look was the best batsman in the world. Bliss
was it in that dawn to be alive, but to be young – and watching Gooch bat at Castle
Park in Colchester – was very heaven.

It seemed that every time Essex left Chelmsford and visited my home town, where
the out-ground sits at the foot of a tree-girt hill, looked over by the Norman keep
and bounded by the river Colne, Gooch was making the scoreboard operator reach
for a third number.

*Good embodied
the decent pre-chav
side of Essex*

In 1991 he made 173 against Northamptonshire, with two sixes sailing over my
head at long-off and on to the bonnet of a red Cortina.

But beating Middlesex was what mattered most. I remember a teacher rushing in
late to our classroom that September and announcing that Essex had bowled our
rivals out for 51 at Chelmsford that morning. Only Gooch (helped by Neil Foster)
could win the toss, ask his opponents to bat and be 202 not out by the close of the
first day. It sealed the title for the fifth time in 13 years.

A year earlier, Gooch's *annus mirabilis*, he made 177 as Essex flayed the Lancashire
attack. Asked to make 348 to win in 54 overs, they came home with six balls to spare,
Gooch falling in sight of victory to that little-known bowler, Mike Atherton.

Gooch's feats in 1990 were mesmerising: 2,746 runs, the most by anyone for 29 years, at an average of 101.70, with 12 hundreds. Jimmy Cook made nine runs more the next year, but at an average of 81.

The astonishing thing is that Gooch achieved this in middle age. Fourteen years earlier, on the day that I was born in the same Leytonstone hospital as Gooch had been, he was making 111 for the county at Old Trafford. The day before his swash-buckling at Castle Park in 1990 Gooch was 37 and he would have another six glorious years before retiring halfway through 1997.

Perhaps it was appropriate that a man who embodied the decent, pre-chav side of Essex, which put hard work ahead of glamour and cherished well-earned rewards, should leave soon after the Conservatives were kicked out of office.

Gooch had been part of the Essex side that won their first silverware in 1979. When Mrs Thatcher was re-elected in 1983, Essex won the Championship again. They won their sixth title in 1992, when a cricket-lover, albeit a Surrey man, was given another term in Downing Street.

My wife is tolerant of my fixation but doesn't fully get it

Gooch was still the best in England in 1996, when he was 56 runs short of making 2,000 in a season for the sixth time. Only two batsmen have reached the mark since but Gooch's achievements should encourage Mark Ramprakash, who turned 37 at the end of last season. After making 2,278 runs at an average of 103.54 last year Ramprakash may yet have an Indian summer to match Gooch's in 1990.

I mean that literally as well as descriptively. Gooch's hundred against Lancashire came two days before the first Test against Mohammad Azharuddin's side at Lord's. I was gripped by this brilliant match as Gooch took guard on the first morning and stayed there for almost two days.

His 333 was boosted by hundreds from Allan Lamb and Robin Smith in a marvel-lous Test match for moustaches. The hairy-lipped brigade had a representative in India, too, as Kapil Dev hit Eddie Hemmings for four sixes in a row to avoid the follow-on.

I might now relish something similar this summer, should Mahendra Dhoni, say, hit Monty Panesar into the Nursery four times on the trot. At 14, though, I felt devastated. Had my hero's innings been for nothing? Surely there would not be time to force a result.

But Gooch had more runs in him. He hit four sixes and 13 fours in two and a half hours to create a declaration that gave England a chance. The bowlers did the rest.

It was probably not on his mind but by making 123 Gooch created a marketing hit. Stuart Surridge released a range of numerically interesting bats, emblazoned with 333, 123 and, for those who could add, 456.

My friend Richard pestered his parents to buy him the Stuart Surridge Turbo 333, which weighed a wrist-aching 3lb 3oz. The first ball he faced with it, he did no more than prod forward; the ball caught the shoulder of the bat and raced for four to third man.

The magic bat made a cameo appearance when I got married last summer. "Wouldn't it be nice," I asked the future Mrs Kidd, "to leave the church under a guard of honour of cricket bats?"

Instead of the anticipated withering look, she agreed and I asked Richard, now my best man, to bring some bats, one of which, it turned out, was the SS Turbo 333. Not that it meant anything to Mrs K as we ducked to pass under its blade. She is tolerant of my fixation but doesn't fully get it.

PATRICK KIDD writes on cricket for *The Times* and is the author of the Line and Length blog on timesonline.co.uk

DARREN GOUGH
by STEPHEN TOMPKINSON

My dazzling mate

**The actor loves Darren Gough for his heart-on-sleeve
heroics and full-on friendship**

I first met Darren Dazzler Goughie Gough briefly in Antigua in 1994. Brian Lara was breaking the batting world record for the first time – Gough was not in the squad – and, thanks to battling centuries by Mike Atherton and Robin Smith, England salvaged a draw.

The first thing that strikes you when you meet Goughie is his sincerity. He is a straight-up-and-downer with a smile as wide as the 22 yards he runs up to and attacks with unerring consistency and panache.

The next year our brave boys set off to prise the Ashes from Mark Taylor's Australia. Warney's hat-trick at Melbourne meant we had to win at Sydney. In the first innings at the SCG Darren got that late inswinger judged to perfection, deceiving and dismissing David Boon and Steve Waugh, neither of whom offered a stroke. His first England five-for came when Taylor dollied one of the cheekiest back-of-the-hand slower balls straight into the youngster's grateful hands. He had earlier scored 51 in what *Wisden* described as a "jaunty innings of village-green innocence and charm".

> People asked, "Who's that lanky idiot
> with Darren Gough?" I have
> rarely been prouder

I met up with him and Tuffers, Gus Fraser and Mike Gatting in their hotel that night. I had seen them the week before on Christmas Day dressed as Yankee Doodle Dandy, The Riddler, Lurch and Henry VIII respectively. After Darren's performance with bat and ball spirits were equally high despite getting only a draw. Then again spirits are generally high when Goughie's around. His charm and enthusiasm are infectious. He also lit up the subsequent one-day series, including an audacious reverse pull for four that had Richie Benaud almost speechless.

He returned my support by coming to cheer me on in *Drop the Dead Donkey* at the London Studios. Later, over dinner at Joe Allen's, he revealed not only his admiration for the TV news show but also his penchant for cheesecake. Another exclusive for Damien Day!

Normally in famous theatre-going restaurants like Joe's it is the actors who turn heads but that night it was "who's that lanky idiot with Darren Gough?" I have rarely been prouder.

Our friendship had strengthened to the extent of best wishes and phone conversations with parents at Darren's growing achievements. The night before Lara scored his 375 I had dinner with Darren and he wrote to my father, also called Brian, on a napkin "Thanks for all your son has taught me". Later, I asked Darren to repeat the message. He duly obliged, then stopped and said, "Oh no, I've put thanks for all your son has bought me." Dad treasures it nonetheless.

Having Goughie's never-say-die attitude was essential for every England fan during the mid-1990s. As the next Ashes down under loomed, I got lucky with work schedules. The BBC had asked me to present one of their *Great Railway Journeys of the World*. An incredible trip on the Eastern & Oriental Express from Singapore through to Bangkok. I said yes, with the proviso that I could stop off in Sydney first for a few days' cricket. I am so grateful they agreed.

The SCG is a beautiful ground and the atmosphere there when Australia entertain the Poms is special. Goughie had already endeared himself to the Aussie crowd four years previously and there was an expectant air whenever he started his run-up. He did not disappoint. In a blistering final spell towards the end of the first day our Darren delivered three unplayable balls that showcased his explosive pace and accuracy. It was as comprehensive and exhilarating a hat-trick as you could wish to see. It is testament to the respect that Darren is held in that every spectator stood up and wildly applauded this remarkable feat.

When my Mam died Darren was straight on the phone to my Dad

No two people were more thrilled for Darren than my Mam and Dad. When they finally got to meet their hero in the Mount Nelson Hotel in Cape Town on England's 1999–2000 winter tour of South Africa they were not disappointed. Both he and Tuffers were charm personified in their England blazers and I think Mam was a little breathless at seeing her Yorkshire idol face to face.

When I was asked to appear on Goughie's *This Is Your Life*, I was one of the 'Do you recognise this voice?' guests. Mam said when she watched it that Darren's face broke out into that trademark grin and said: "It's the big 'un." She was thrilled to bits.

Sadly Mam passed away suddenly in 2004. When Darren heard, he was straight on the phone to my Dad to offer his sympathy and share memories of meeting her. It was something above and beyond the call of duty and meant so much to my father, my brother and me. We will never be able to thank him enough for his sincerity and kindness.

The next time I saw Goughie he had traded in his whites for white tie and tails. I'd come to support him in the final of *Strictly Come Dancing*. My daughter Daisy and I had been watching and rooting for him every week. I couldn't miss the final. KP and I were in the audience as twinkle-toes won over the nation's voters by encompassing the spirit of the show with his heart on his sleeve, just as he always did on the cricket field.

As a player he would knock himself out for you as he proved emphatically at Lord's after taking a brilliant catch in the deep and smashing his head into the turf. I count myself fortunate to call him a friend. I wish all the very best to him and his family as he approaches retirement.

STEPHEN TOMPKINSON is an actor, best known as star of *Drop the Dead Donkey*, *Ballykissangel*, *Brassed Off* and *Wild at Heart*, and a Chance to shine ambassador (www.chancetoshine.org)

DAVID GOWER
by ELEANOR OLDROYD

The day that launched two careers

When David Gower pulled his first ball in Test cricket for four, his was not the only life about to change, remembers Eleanor Oldroyd

Friday June 2, 1978. It was a big day for English cricket . . . and a big day for me. It was my 16th birthday. I got only one card in the post but after breakfast my parents, my two brothers and I got in the car to drive to Birmingham. On the way we stopped in Kidderminster where my brothers bought me *Abbey Road* by The Beatles. We then made our way to Edgbaston, where Pakistan were due to resume on 162 for 9.

The reason I know all this in such detail, 31 years later, is that I recently found, hidden in a box in the corner of the loft, a grey school exercise book – my diary of the summer of '78, my first tentative foray into the world of sports journalism.

I recorded that Chris Old had taken four wickets in five balls the previous day. "Wicket, wicket, no ball, wicket, wicket! Incredible!" That Brearley and Wood opened for England – Wood was out first, lbw, and Brearley was run out soon after – followed by the moment that I can picture so clearly, without the help of a teenage diary.

"Then Gower came in and hooked his first ball in Test cricket for 4! He proceeded to make a super 58, with some beautiful strokes. It really was a pleasure to watch – I'm sure I'm privileged to have seen it."

> He had pure, unadulterated talent and disregard for stuffiness and convention

To those who are now insisting it was a pull, not a hook, I say in my defence that I was new to the technicalities of the game. Two years earlier I had been captivated by the magnificence of Viv Richards, Andy Roberts and Michael Holding, the grit of Bob Woolmer, David Steele and Dennis Amiss in that sizzling summer of '76.

I told my parents I no longer wanted to read *Jackie* magazine and they took out a subscription to *The Cricketer* for me instead. So I was no mere dilettante, no giggling girl swooning at the blond curls and pale blue eyes of DI Gower. I was an aficionado of his elegant late cut and languid leg glance (once I'd worked out what to call them).

Pulling power: Gower hits his first ball in Test cricket, from Pakistan's Liaqat Ali, for four in 1978

Five years on I was studying Modern Languages at Cambridge, although Fenner's was a fatal temptation from essays on Molière and Goethe. My journalistic ambitions had developed, too; and as sports editor of the student newspaper *Stop Press* I could choose my own assignments.

So when Leicestershire rolled into town for a gentle early-season work-out, I plucked up courage to approach Gower for a chat. He "didn't see why not" (according to the summer 1983 volume of the diary), and thus I found myself armed with tape recorder and notepad, sitting on a rainy Cambridge day conducting my first real, grown-up interview.

He was "pleasant, chatty and relaxing", confiding that he was finding the newly acquired press interest hard to deal with.

"The intrusion comes when the phone keeps ringing; it's a cross between good and bad, because it's good when you're the centre of attention but it's a pain when the phone goes again and it's another bloke wanting the same opinion."

Looking back now, I realise he gave me great quotes – no patronising of the rookie student journalist. He was frank about the disappointment of losing the Ashes the previous winter, honest about his ambition to be England captain one day and

thoughtful about the desirability of extending county matches to four days rather than three.

When the rain stopped next day he scored the opening first-class century of the season, against the "demoralised" CU bowlers. But between my interview and that ton is a tale which, for many, sums up the man. "Gower's century was all the more remarkable as it took place after a late-night dip in the Cam [I wrote]. He made his acquaintance with its murky waters on Monday night on a punting trip with other members of the Leicestershire team. Undergraduate-style horseplay from his team-mates dislodged the England batting star from his position on the end of the punt."

And maybe this is what makes David Gower my favourite cricketer: pure, unadulterated talent, of course; a healthy disregard for stuffiness and convention. Doesn't buzzing the wicket in a Tiger Moth during a tour match in Australia make the Fredalo incident look puny? But behind it all, a professionalism for which he did not always get proper credit. Eighteen centuries and over 8,000 Test runs in a career that fizzled out over a personality clash hardly suggest a man unwilling to apply himself.

He makes broadcasting look easy – just as he did batting

And of all the sportsmen-turned-broadcasters, he has to be one of the finest: laconic and witty as a commentator but utterly professional. I saw him a couple of years ago at The Oval perfecting the walking piece to camera while going down a flight of steps in front of a mildly inebriated crowd willing him to trip up. He made it look easy – just as he did batting.

To refresh my memory with footage of some of those beautifully poised, effortless strokes I went on to YouTube. Surely they would have the double hundred against Australia in 1985? Or even that famous shot off Liaqat Ali in '78? But no. "David Gower and Jonathan Ross Feel a Female Bodybuilder", from the late and not very lamented *They Think It's All Over*, springs to the top of the list.

So I think I'll stick to my own memories of the day I turned 16 – and had two significant presents. I still love *Abbey Road*, and David Gower is still my favourite cricketer.

ELEANOR OLDROYD is a BBC Five Live sports presenter

TOM GRAVENEY
by FRANK KEATING

Too lordly for Lord's

He was the most carefree batsman of his generation, but it was all too much for the selectors. Frank Keating recalls the genial strokeplay of 'Our Tom'

The first time is always the best – and for romantics anyway, as the years roll on, the first remains the most enduringly gratifying for mind and spirit. I talk, of course, of hero worship. Recollection warms the memory as well, for you are seldom betrayed by the figure you first lionised in the uncomplicated purity of early childhood. In my case, I am even more fortunate – my boyhood's callow wide-eyed idol worship has grown into a fond and comradely relationship, man-to-man, ancient-to-ancient. When I was 12, Tom Graveney was 10 years older and already a champion folk hero of Gloucestershire in England's pastoral and cuddly West Country. Now he is 77 and I talk to him as a contemporary. And my hair is greyer even than his.

Yet I am still in schoolboy awe of the valorous chivalry of his deeds at cricket, of the genuine creative invention and authentic artistry of his transcendent batsmanship.

Gloucestershire, of course, had a noble heritage in batsmanship. It was the county of Grace, and of Jessop and Hammond, too. In the south was the city of Bristol, where the county cricketers were based, but once a midsummer they would travel north into the blissful hills to play two or three Championship matches in the stately town of Cheltenham. This visit would be midsummer's high-temperature mark for us local urchins, as well as our fathers and uncles, sisters, cousins and aunts. Everyone all around was "on holiday for the cricket".

August 1950 held the most red-hot two days of my sheltered life so far, when the county gathered to play the mesmerising West Indian tourists at Cheltenham. Of course, our fellows were skittled in no time – and in successive innings – by the ravenous and magical guiles of those spin "twins" Sonny Ramadhin and Alf Valentine. The only one of our batsmen to play the two wizards of tweak with any remote degree of certainty was "our Tom" – fresh country-boy's hale face, coltishly upright and gangly shy at the crease, but with a high twirly back-lift and a stirring signature-flourish in the follow-through of his trademark cover-drive (a stroke which would become a timeless artefact of serene and mellow beauty around the world and throughout the game). And a man sitting, sardined, on the grass next to me in the rapt, packed throng said: "Our Tom'll be servin' England within a twelvemonth, you'll see."

And so he was, and so we did. He was blooded for one Test against the South Africans in 1951 at Old Trafford on a sticky and he stayed in for an hour to make 15 ("full of cultured promise," said John Arlott on the wireless), and that October set sail

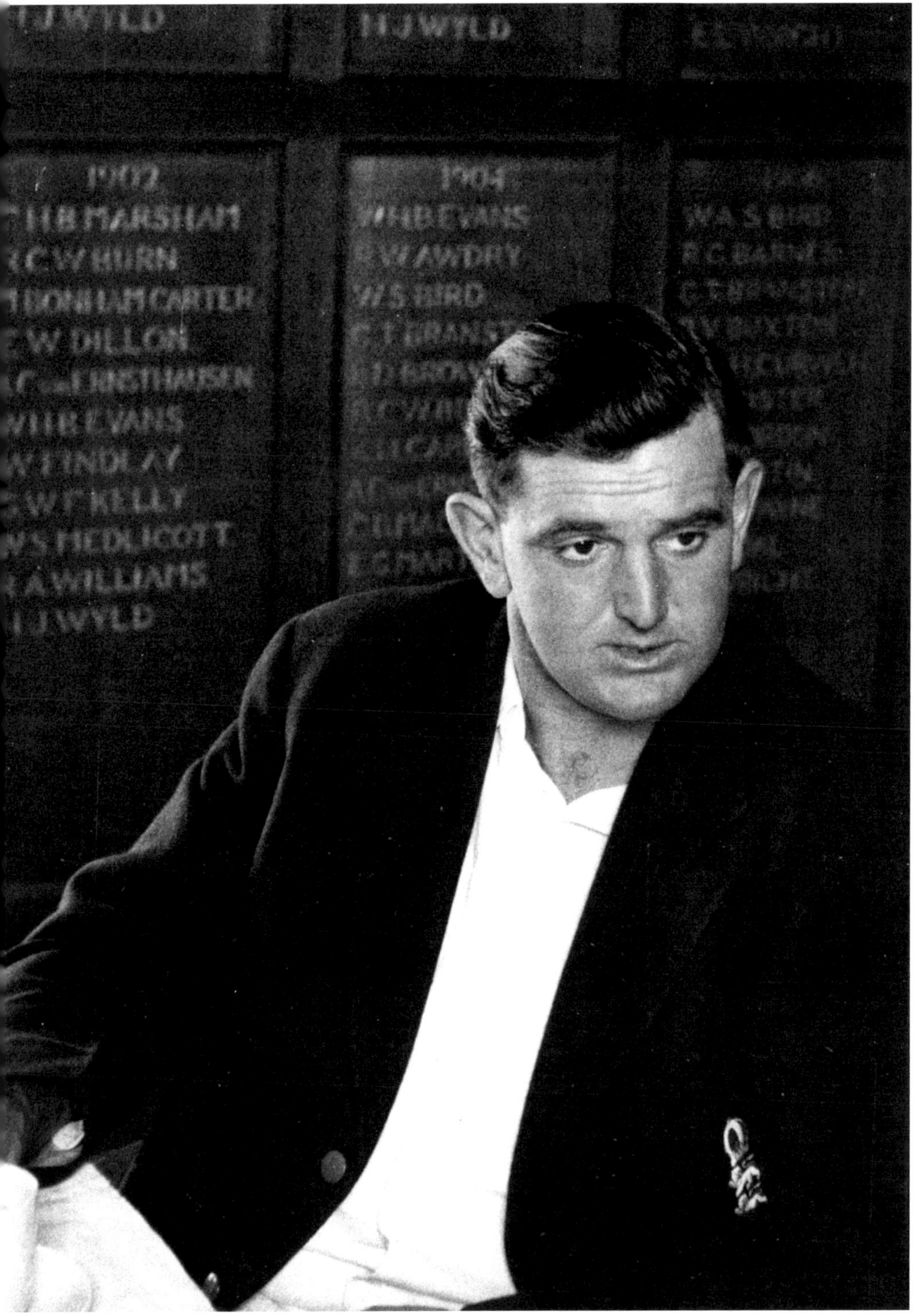
H.J.WYLD
1902
1904
W.H.B.EVANS
W.S.BIRD

on the liner Chusan for his first overseas MCC tour to take in the new sights, sounds, and differing surfaces (either coir [coconut] matting, jute, or turf) of 'All India'.

At once, he scored warm-up centuries at Bombay and Dehra Dun – a whole county back home straining its ears around the wireless sets in their kitchens enthralled by his progress – but he missed the first Test match in Delhi with a severe bash of dysentery. A week in the Hindu Rao hospital got him over the worst, but he was still uneasily queasy when the second Test came along at Bombay. More than 50 years on, he remembers: "I was still feeling groggy, but was determined to play. I reckon I felt and looked like a skeleton when I walked in to bat." He took a pint of water and a salt tablet every half hour, which turned into an awful lot of water and salt – because he endured for eight and a quarter hours in the fierce heat against the craft and cunning of Amarnath, Shinde and Mankad, and the young man's epic 175 was to remain the highest Test score by an Englishman in India until Dennis Amiss made 179 against Bedi, Chandra and Venkat fully 25 years later.

Us hero-worshippers continued to raise the rafters back in Gloucestershire as Tom served England with grace and charm for the next 10 years – first the colt matching the elderly monarchs Hutton and Compton, stroke for stroke, then the two lordly and haughty amateurs, May and Cowdrey. By which time a group of dullard "industrial" selectors at Lord's became grudging . . . this Graveney, they said was all very well, but, horrors, he treats Test cricket like festival cricket, his manner is too carefree and smiling, his strokeplay too genial that he only seeks to present his great ability rather than enforce it ruthlessly.

So England dropped him for five of the next six years, and Tom moved across the border to play for Worcester, still a legend in his own locality and where the mellow architecture of his glorious strokeplay matched the imperishable resplendence of the ancient cathedral which adjoins the county's famous ground.

Graveney continued to enchant all England every summer, but not the England Test team. Till, in 1966, another string of sad England performances had a brave new batch of selectors seeing sense and turning, once again, to Graveney – now in his 40th year – to dig them out of a deep hole being dug by Sobers' dashing West Indians. At Lord's, too. Tom counter-attacked and answered the ferocity of Hall and Griffith with a majestic 96 – then 109 in the following Test, and an even more regal 165 in the one after that at The Oval. He was back, and it was not only Gloucestershire amd Worcestershire now who were revelling in the joy of it. All cricket was under the spell of his masterclasses. The following summer, against India at Lord's, Graveney beguilingly unrolled another masterpiece – 151 against Chandra, Bedi, and Prasanna – "superb," said *Wisden*, "the day belonged entirely to Graveney, elegant as ever."

In the New Year honours list of 1968, the Queen awarded him the OBE and he celebrated with a sublime 118 against West Indies at Port-of-Spain – his favourite century of all his career 122. Henry Blofeld, who was there, said "any art gallery in the world would have bought that innings for millions". The following winter, Graveney's 105 against Pakistan at Karachi rounded off the enchanted oddyssey.

The hero still lives in Cheltenham, where it all began. We still take a beer together, and I sit at his feet and listen, rapt again as the schoolboy was. Content and smiling,

Our Tom: Graveney during his 164 against West Indies at The Oval in 1957

still hale and hail-fellow, Tom has had both hips replaced, but still plays regular golf and keenly follows his beloved cricket (he thinks modern bats far too "blunderbuss" heavy – "only a tiny minority, a Lara or a Tendulkar can use them as we did, like a rapier, a wand").

When he retired from the crease in his mid-40s (4,882 Test runs and 47,793 first-class), the wise old cricket writer JM Kilburn hurrahed Graveney's uninhibited heroic approach: "In an age preoccupied by accountancy, he has given the game warmth and colour and inspiration far beyond the tally of the scorebook."

Precisely. The batsmanship of Our Tom was of the orchard rather than the forest, blossom susceptible to frost but breathing in the sunshine. Taking enjoyment as it came, he gave enjoyment which still warms the winters of memory.

FRANK KEATING grew up in the West Country and is one of its best-loved sportswriters. He is a former chief sports writer of *The Guardian* and still writes for the paper

WES HALL
by TONY COZIER

From fire to friendship

**Tony Cozier faced Wes Hall and lived to tell the tale –
and many more besides as a life-long association developed**

When I first laid eyes on Wes Hall he was in the next parish. As I scratched my guard
the bowler in the far distance at the end of a run that would become as identifiable as
any in the game was the latest West Indies tearaway.

I was the 17-year-old opening batsman for the Lodge School at a time when the
three top secondary schools in Barbados were part of the highest division of domestic
cricket, along with clubs that routinely included Test and first-class players (presum-
ably it was supposed to be character building). He was 20, immense and with the
chiselled physique of the light-heavyweight boxer his father was.

Only a few months earlier he had been hurling them down, at appreciable pace
but without much control, for West Indies on their 1957 tour of England. He had
converted from keeping wickets to knocking them over only a couple of years earlier
on leaving Combermere (along with Harrison College cricket's other favoured school
in Barbados).

> He quickly pricked
> my pride: "You lucky
> you still living!"

He was said to be erratic and prone to no-balls. Neither claim lifted our confidence
for, whatever else, he was decidedly quick. If he was not sure where the next ball
would go, we certainly were not and, since the back-foot law was still in operation,
he was pretty much stepping on the batsman's toes every time he dragged.

Somehow, through youthful eyesight, reflexes, bravado, luck, whatever, I clipped
a boundary through square leg in the opening over on the way to a scintillating 24.
The image has justifiably remained with me, as sharp as if on a high-definition TV
screen. When, by now old friends, I felt comfortable enough to mention it to Wes a
few months back, he quickly pricked my pride: "You lucky you still living!"

Thankfully I never had to face him again. The next time I saw him in the flesh
was in the Caribbean against India in 1961–62. He had developed into one of the

most feared bowlers in international cricket and I was safely settled in the press box, relishing the thrill of that galloping approach, that explosive delivery, that menacing follow-through, that flying crucifix around the neck that I had first experienced from 22 yards, or considerably less, five years earlier.

In the interim I had shivered through Canadian winters, blithely distracted from university studies by reports on crackling shortwave reception that told of the coming of age of a raft of new stars under the guidance of Frank Worrell: Sobers, Kanhai, Hunte, Nurse, Gibbs and, of course, Hall.

As one of the few West Indian journalists following the team in the subsequent years of dominance and in an era when players did not take a critical reference to a poor shot or a wayward spell as a personal insult, I developed friendships with most of those legends. It was most natural with Wes.

It was not long before I came to appreciate what CLR James had immediately observed. "Hall simply exudes good nature at every pore," he wrote in *Beyond A Boundary*. It might seem a contradiction for, as James also noted, "Hall merely puts his head down and let's you have it, and it's pretty hot!" Yet it is a virtue that has never changed.

This is not to say it was his only characteristic. There was a wholehearted energy and enjoyment in everything he did, an obvious sense of fun, vividly captured on the black-and-white footage of the 1960–61 tied Test in Brisbane featuring his famous frenetic last over and, not least, his equally frenetic half-century.

Wes is renowned for his entertaining, if often prolonged, oratory

After that series the Australian commentator Johnnie Moyes described Wes as "a rare box-office attraction, a man who caught and held the affections of the paying public". So it has been throughout a life of several intriguing incarnations.

After a couple of car crashes and the exhaustion of giving his all for several teams around the world took their toll and the "pace like fire" (the appropriate title of his autobiography) was extinguished, he took the usual path of retired players, into administration as selector, team manager and, eventually, board president. Poor health caused his resignation but, well again, he is once more involved, now as part of Allen Stanford's 20/20 revolution.

But there is more to Wes Hall than cricket. He entered politics in his 40s, spending 10 years as a Barbados cabinet minister and, more recently, turned to the church to become a minister of a different kind, a legacy of a deeply religious upbringing.

They were all connections from which I benefited. Wes was regularly my 'reliable source' on complicated cricket issues and I was chuffed when he agreed to officiate at the weddings of both our children although I was careful to emphasise the need to keep the service short and to remind him of the time as Wes is renowned for his entertaining, if often prolonged, oratory as well as for his tardiness.

His myriad cricket tales, embellished with highfalutin words as long as his run-up, are guaranteed to leave audiences convulsed in laughter, however many times they have heard them before. His description of that last tied Test over is one of the after-dinner classics.

If he happens to be a little late, he is always worth waiting for. When he turned up at my 50th birthday bash at 1am, numbers were beginning to thin. Wes kept it going for another four hours.

TONY COZIER is the definitive voice of West Indies cricket, writing about and commentating on the game in the Caribbean for 50 years

GRAEME HICK
by SIMON HATTENSTONE

The shy and retiring run machine

Graeme Hick finally called it a day, when Simon Hattenstone, a Hick obsessive, said it was time to celebrate achievement not missed opportunity

No sportsman has got to me quite like Graeme Hick. It is not just the depth of emotions he has inspired; it is the variety. He is the ultimate enigma wrapped in a riddle wrapped in a whopping great paradox.

As a young man – a boy really – Hicky broke pretty much every record that was there for the breaking. Twenty years ago he scored 1,000 runs before the end of May, including 405 not out against Somerset. He was the youngest player to score 2,000 runs in a season, the youngest to hit 50 centuries and the second youngest to reach a hundred hundreds.

This broad-shouldered, silent hulk arrived from Zimbabwe a month before his 18th birthday in 1984 with little more than a cricket bat for company. When he finally qualified for England in 1991 after seven years, he was going to be its saviour.

He did not bat with the grace of a Gower or the swashbuckling charisma of a Richards. He simply stood there, straight-backed, stared at the ball, waited for a bad 'un and smacked it to the boundary. He scored his runs quickly but he was never truly thrilling. What he had in spades was judgement, patience and a pair of mighty arms. Hick was a farmer's son and there was something appropriately rustic about the way he would raise his bat scythe-like and smite the ball. He was also a decent spin bowler and a brilliant slip fielder.

On the eve of his Test debut (a debut shared by that other great enigma Mark Ramprakash) Brough Scott wrote: "The promise is so fresh and so infinite that there is also a touch of sadness about it."

It was a prescient comment. He scored six in each innings. By August he had been dropped having scored 75 runs at 10.71. He was dropped in virtually every series he played after that. He was dismissed as a softy by those who should have known better. The England coach Ray Illingworth called him a cry-baby after he was dropped yet again. Some dismissed him as a flat-track bully, said he couldn't play the true quicks and scoffed at his suspect temperament and lack of technique.

Me, I just cursed the way such a talent had been destroyed by poor management. I still believe he could have had a Test average in the fifties if only those in authority had put an arm round his shoulder and kept the faith.

It was not just Illingworth who mistreated him. During the 1994–95 Ashes tour, when he was 98 not out and battling his way back into form against Australia in

Sydney, Mike Atherton (a caring man in every other way) declared, accusing him of scoring too slowly. Hick was too good-natured to hold a grudge but the pain and shame of being stopped on 98 stayed with him forever. He once told me: "I regard Athers as a good friend but I wouldn't have minded a good thump at him."

After his Test failures he would go home to Worcester, where everybody adored him, put his head down, pile on the centuries, return to the England fold and disappoint again. There were successes. He scored six Test hundreds and averaged 31 – disappointing certainly but not horrendous.

But ultimately for a man of such immense ability he failed at Test level. And the more he failed, the more devoted I became to him. In 2002 I interviewed him for *Wisden Cricket Monthly*. What moved me about him most was his honesty. He might be notoriously shy, he might hate interviews but I have never heard a sportsman speak so openly and eloquently. It soon became obvious how much he had been misunderstood. Despite his reserve he was an emotional man. Just watching his kids at sports day left him in tears.

He told me how he had been to a psychologist who said that to move on he had first to admit to someone close to him that he felt he had failed as a Test cricketer.

He smiled sheepishly as he explained how he gathered the strength, gulped out his confession and his friend continued waffling on as if he had not heard what Hick had told him.

He said that he had finally learned to enjoy the successes and stop torturing himself over the things that did not go to plan. His most important innings for England? Scoring 40 for England in Karachi to help clinch the series against Pakistan in 2000–01.

Hick loved scoring runs but he was the polar opposite of Geoffrey Boycott. If anything he could have done with more ego. This was six years ago. We were in the changing room, a storm was blowing up outside and the day was closing in. So, it seemed, was his career.

Rather than focusing on what could have been, we should celebrate a remarkable career

After all, he was already 36. But he was determined to go on. It was as if he hoped that somehow his astonishing success at county level would eventually erase the disappointments of his Test career. After a couple of fallow years he started hitting centuries for fun again – in his forties.

He proved himself an immense Twenty20 player and says he may play on in this format in India. As for the first-class game he leaves with an average of 52 plus and 136 centuries, which places him eighth on the all-time list of century-makers. In all cricket he is the second most prolific run-scorer, behind Graham Gooch, passing 64,000 runs this summer.

Rather than focusing on what could have been, it is time to celebrate what has been a truly remarkable career.

SIMON HATTENSTONE is a feature writer for the *Guardian*

ERIC HOLLIES
by MICHAEL BILLINGTON

The jolliest party pooper

Eric Hollies is best known for keeping Bradman's Test average under 100 but being an unwitting spoilsport belies the truth of a smiling leggie, says Michael Billington

Eric Hollies has an assured place in cricket history: as the party pooper of all time. And although it's a story every cricket lover knows, it bears retelling. The date is August 14, 1948 and Don Bradman is making his final Test appearance, needing only four runs to achieve an average of 100. As Bradman makes his way to the wicket, The Oval rises. In the middle the English captain, Norman Yardley, raises his cap, calls for three cheers and then shakes the Don by the hand. The crowd falls silent in expectation. Bradman takes his guard and Hollies bowls him an orthodox leg-spinner. The next ball, a googly, is pitched slightly further up. It draws Bradman forward, he misses it and looks back to find his stumps shattered – the great man departs: "bowled Hollies 0."

There are many ways of looking at that historic event. As an eight-year-old, living in the heart of Warwickshire, my ear was clamped to the radio, where John Arlott apparently spoke for the nation. "I wonder," said Arlott, "if you see a ball very clearly in your last Test in England, on a ground where you've played some of the biggest cricket of your life, and where the opposing side has just stood round you and given you three cheers, and the crowd has clapped you all the way to the wicket. I wonder if you really see the ball at all." And Len Hutton added to the myth as he quoted Bradman saying: "It's not easy to bat with tears in your eyes."

But we, in Warwickshire, had a different view. We knew that our man Hollies, the most cunning spin bowler in England, was simply too good for Bradman. We also subsequently found out that Hollies, who had bowled Bradman 10 days earlier in a county game where he took eight Australian first-innings wickets for 107, was working to a plan: "I'll bowl the googly second ball," Hollies told Tom Dollery before leaving for The Oval, "just in case he's expecting it first one." As for the theory that emotion overcame Bradman, Jack Crapp, who was fielding at first slip, seemed to demolish that when he told Frank Keating: "That bugger Bradman never had a tear in his eye his whole life!"

Whatever the truth, Hollies was always my schoolboy hero: not so much because of his deeds for England as for the way he played cricket for Warwickshire. He was the ultimate pro, regularly bowling well over 1,000 overs a summer. Long before Shane Warne was born, Hollies showed that a leggie could combine devastating accuracy with guile: astonishing to think that in a long, war-interrupted career that

lasted from 1932 to 1957 Hollies conceded only 2.23 runs an over. But, above all, there was an innate cheerfulness about Eric Hollies. Again like Warne – though without highlights – he was a stockily rotund, fair-haired figure who looked as if bowling was a pleasure and nature's gift not a punishment. As Cardus once said of Johnny Briggs, the Lancashire bowler: "He had just to show his face and a light passed over the field and with it a companionable warmth."

Nowhere was Hollies' humour more apparent than in his batting. He was one of the game's legendary rabbits who in his first-class career took more wickets (2,323) than he scored runs (1,673); it's a melancholy thought that he wouldn't stand an earthly of getting into today's multi-skilled England side. But I can still hear the ironic roar that greeted Hollies every time he came out to bat. His walk to the wicket was a mock-triumphal progress. On reaching the crease, he would solemnly pat the wicket – in those days always uncovered and occasionally bumpy – with the back of his bat, in imitation of a real batsman. On one famous occasion at Worcester, finding all the

Party pooper: Hollies bowling at The Oval in the final Ashes Test of 1948 when he bowled Bradman for a duck

fielders clustered close for his arrival, he handed his bat to the umpire and unobtrusively crouched down in the leg-trap.

Humour was also for Hollies a form of protection. He had a spasmodic career for England, first playing against West Indies on the 1934–35 tour. And, after his heroic deeds at The Oval in 1948, he played against the New Zealanders in 1949 and West Indies in 1950. That, and another brilliant Warwickshire season where he took 117 wickets at 18.13, led to his selection for the 1950–51 tour of Australia and New Zealand. But he was constantly passed over for the Tests in favour of the kangaroo-hopping leggie Doug Wright. One baking-hot day at Sydney, ignored by his skipper Freddie Brown and fielding down by the Hill, the locals barracked Hollies. "What's the matter – don't they bury their dead in Birmingham?" someone shouted. "No, they stuff 'em and send 'em out to Australia," was Hollies' reply; and from that moment he had the Hill in the palm of his hand.

I can still
see now the
Hollies smile

But I like to remember Hollies in his pomp, in the great 1951 Championship-winning Warwickshire side. He took 145 wickets that memorable summer and, with his Brearleyesque captain Tom Dollery, was the team's linchpin. I can still see now the Hollies smile, the deceptively slow amble up to the crease, the ingenious mix of orthodox legbreaks, topspinners and googlies. And I recall one particular, late-July match against Yorkshire where Hollies took nine wickets in all and where the aggregate attendance, according to *Wisden*, was an astonishing 43,000. That was the county game at its best; and for me Eric Hollies, affable as Falstaff yet full of the leggie's cerebral cunning, was the perfect embodiment of the winning spirit of Warwickshire cricket.

MICHAEL BILLINGTON is drama critic of *The Guardian* and a life-long Warwickshire supporter

LEN HUTTON
by DAVID NOBBS

Raising the bar

His schoolfriends all adored Compton or Edrich but for David Nobbs it had to be Len Hutton, the master technician who made himself into a stylist

There was never any choice in the matter. Len Hutton had to be my childhood hero.

I first came across him when I was three, although I didn't realise it at the time. We were having lunch in my grandparents' dark dining room in rural Essex. The room smelt of silence and Gorgonzola cheese. That day, however, the silence was broken by the wireless. I remember the slow, measured tones of the commentator, then a burst of excitement. Many years later I deduced that I had been listening to Hutton making his world record 364 at The Oval.

The war came and went. It was 1946. I was 11, and my Uncle Kenneth took me to my first cricket match – Surrey versus Yorkshire, again at The Oval. We sat on a wooden bench, right at the back, under the gasometer. There was a good crowd. Surrey were dismissed for not much more than 100, with the Yorkshire spinner Robinson taking eight wickets. By the close of play, Yorkshire had struggled to 150 for 5. Hutton was playing on a different surface from everybody else. They were on an awkward slow turner with variable bounce. He was batting on a billiard table. He was 91 not out. He was a god.

In 1947 England thrashed South Africa. Compton and Edrich carried all before them. Hutton failed to reach 30 in six innings. I was at school in Kent. All the boys worshipped Compton and Edrich. Only I, stubbornly, faithfully, stood up for Hutton. His failures darkened my summer.

He came good in the fourth Test at Leeds, sharing an opening stand of 141 with Washbrook and going on to make a century. The sun was shining again.

In 1948 things got worse. He seemed nervous against Lindwall and Miller. The selectors dropped him for the third Test. People were saying that he wasn't the player he had been before the war, that an injury in the gym, involving a slight shortening of one arm, had affected his technique.

The selectors replaced him with George Emmett of Gloucestershire. I didn't hate Emmett – it wasn't his fault – but how I hated those selectors. Now I was in a real quandary. I wanted us to do well against Australia, of course I did, but how I wanted Emmett to fail.

He duly failed, Hutton returned at Leeds with scores of 81 and 57. I listened to the fifth Test on holiday in Swansea. England batted first. Len made 30. Not brilliant? The next highest scorer was Norman Yardley with seven. England were dismissed for 52.

In 1950 I was allowed into a pub for the first time, in the tiny village of Little Yeldham in Essex. The pub had a TV, and our family didn't, so my cousin John, 11, and I, 15, sat in a tiny darkened room in the Stone and Faggot and watched a tiny TV set. Again, the venue was The Oval. West Indies had made more than 500. England struggled, dismissed for 344. Again, Hutton seemed to have brought his own pitch. He carried his bat for 202. Of course he did. I was watching.

In 1952 he became the first professional cricketer to captain England. The world was changing. In 1953, Hutton's England attempted to regain the Ashes. The first four Tests were drawn. At The Oval Australia won the toss and made 275. England responded with 306 (Hutton 82). I went to the last two days of that historic match. I saw Australia begin their second innings brightly. Hutton, that cautious Yorkshireman, had spin on at both ends by the time the score reached 20. There was near hysteria in the ground as Lock and Laker reduced Australia from 59 for 1 to 61 for 5.

Needing 132 to win, Hutton ran himself out for 17; he was mortal after all, but we won by eight wickets and ran across the ground to celebrate in front of the pavilion. Hutton lost the toss in every Test, but won the Ashes. Of course he did. I was there.

In Australia, in 1954–55, Hutton at last won the toss, put Australia in, saw them score 601 and win by an innings and 154 runs. Did I panic? Yes, utterly. Hutton didn't. This time he pinned his faith on pace, and we won the next three Tests.

What a record the man had but it wasn't just the results that thrilled me. He was a joy to watch. He had great economy of style. I recall the effortless ease of his leg-side strokes, the perfection of his late cuts, the glorious freedom of his cover drive, nose over bat, bat almost stroking pad. He wasn't tall, he didn't have the willowy elegance of a Graveney, but his sheer technical perfection elevated him into a stylist. If a cricket manual had come to life, it would have been Len Hutton.

He could be exciting too. I remember watching him charging down the wicket to hammer Roly Jenkins, the Worcestershire legspinner, through the covers with savage elegance. It was magic.

They say that his most astonishing innings was his 62 not out, on an unplayable (to everyone else) Brisbane 'stickie' in 1950. Again, it was as if he had taken his own pitch with him.

Many years after his knighthood and his death, I went out with a Yorkshire lady, who had lived in Pudsey.

"Hutton," she said. "Oh, I knew Len Hutton. He was a friend of my uncle. He used to come to our house."

I paused.

"Will you marry me?" I said. What else could I have said?

She did, incidentally. Of course she did. I was there.

DAVID NOBBS is the creator and writer of *The Fall and Rise of Reginald Perrin* and the Henry Pratt series

World record: Hutton leaves The Oval after his 364 against Australia in 1938

DOUGLAS JARDINE
by CHRISTOPHER DOUGLAS

An irresistible force

Douglas Jardine's desire to win back the Ashes at all costs brought him the urn and vilification in England and Australia. Which is why Christopher Douglas loves him

It's a perverse choice, I know, because DRJ wasn't exactly a crowd pleaser – dour, defensive batting style, awkward, stiff-legged way of moving around the field and a firm belief that any noise coming from the stands should be punished by an immediate 30-minute suspension of play. He captained England only 15 times (won 9, lost 1, drew 5) but as time goes by his stature seems to grow. And that's because in 1932–33 he took a side to Australia and regained the Ashes. Ray Illingworth and Pelham Warner are the only other England captains to have achieved this.

Douglas Jardine is the name more than any other that stands for the legendary British qualities of cool-headed determination, implacable resolve, patrician disdain for crowds and critics alike – if you're English that is. To Australians the name is synonymous with the legendary British qualities of snobbishness, cynicism and downright Pommie arrogance.

I certainly don't spend time re-reading accounts of matches that Douglas Jardine played or watching old film of him, nor do I have his photo on my bedroom wall. But, since writing a biography of him over 20 years ago, I have always had an affection for him, not just as a fearless, single-minded, scary, hook-nosed sort of toff which I suppose part of me would quite like to be, but because he was partly responsible for my education.

I left school at 15 and the two years I spent in my early twenties researching DRJ's life and trying to express it in coherent form was the nearest I got to going to college. There wasn't much money in it so I had to subsidise the writing with scraps of TV acting work and doing the horses (I dedicated the book to my five biggest winners). It's safe to say I would have been the very last person DRJ would have chosen for the job.

I was deeply conscious of my unsuitability as I interviewed those who knew him: Percy Fender, Gubby Allen, Jack Fingleton, Bob Wyatt and so on. But having to get to grips with the single most important episode in DRJ's life – Bodyline – with very little prior knowledge still less opinion was probably an advantage.

The defenders of bodyline bowling have all died off and we are all now agreed that it had to end but the more interesting thing about it to me is that it had to start. It's true that Jardine was the first to implement the strategy of fast short-pitched bowling with a packed leg-side field, but it was a stage in the game's evolution rather than a dastardly one-off plan and it was always going to happen sooner or later. The lbw law, the pitches, the height of the stumps, even the size of the ball were all in the batsman's favour at the time and something had to give. Even Don Bradman, bodyline's chief target, admitted as much in a letter to MCC shortly before the tour.

There was nothing illegal about bodyline. DRJ had such a profound respect for the laws that he would never have countenanced it otherwise. It wasn't by any means guaranteed to work but he was prepared to risk everything on its success – death or glory. He called his account of the tour In Quest of the Ashes (it's just been splendidly reissued by Methuen with a brilliant foreword on Bodyline by Mike Brearley) and he saw the campaign as something noble and knightly. "Fear and be slain" he would quote to his children in later life, and on the Bodyline tour his bowlers would be reminded as they enjoyed a final fag before taking the field that "an hour of glorious life is worth an age without a name".

> ## His status as a sporting icon seems more secure than ever

He wasn't a villain but decades of Australian resentment have lent him a kind of villainous glamour that I find irresistible. Likewise his sense of humour: when Herbert Sutcliffe had a benefit match coming up DRJ sent him an umbrella for luck.

Until recently his portrait hung in the Long Room at Lord's, appropriately enough underneath Bradman's, DRJ's cool gaze staring directly into the faces of visiting teams as they clattered through the hushed interior on their way out on to the field. He has been moved to the bar now, as has Bradman, which I think is a pity because it always seemed gloriously ironic that the two great adversaries – the master strategist and the game's pre-eminent genius – should occupy the same patch of wall space. But Douglas Jardine has survived many attempts to airbrush him out of history and now his status as a sporting icon seems more secure than ever.

CHRISTOPHER DOUGLAS is an actor and writer best known in cricket circles as the co-creator of Dave Podmore, the fictional journeyman cricketer who inhabits The Guardian and BBC Radio 4

ALAN KNOTT
by MARK POUGATCH

The eccentricities of genius

Mark Pougatch loved Alan Knott for his uniqueness – and his hankie

Headingley 1981 was a Test match that immortalised Ian Botham in the eyes of so many teenagers that he's still their cricket hero a quarter of a century later. For lovers of English fast bowling, it was Bob Willis's finest hour and they argue his achievements are too easily overlooked. For one 13-year-old growing up in East Sussex, though, it was a match which reaffirmed that, good as Bob Taylor was with the gloves, his batting wasn't up to it, and England had to bring their No. 1 wicketkeeper back into the side.

Alan Knott was England's undisputed keeper between his Test debut in 1967 and the Packer affair that split the cricket world a decade later. In that time he played in 89 of England's 93 Tests – a testament to his durability, fitness, dedication and all-round startling ability. Knott the cricketer was in many ways a one-off. Whereas Taylor might have been the keeper easier on the eye and more orthodox, Knott developed his own style, taking the ball on his knees when he could have stayed on his feet and catching the ball one-handed more than budding keepers are taught to do. His batting was even more idiosyncratic. He could sweep spinners to distraction, never minded chipping the ball over the infield, changed his grip when he thought it appropriate and in 95 Tests averaged just under 33 with five centuries and 30 fifties.

> His initials APE were
> in keeping with simian,
> craggy looks

It was Knott the keeper that made such an impression on my young mind. My father was a mad keen cricketer and, although we lived in Sussex, he was a Kent member. He wanted to use a field in the village in which we lived for his wandering team called The Grannies, which this summer celebrates its 50th anniversary. Dad wrote to both counties asking for advice from the groundsman but only Kent replied so he became a member there. As I started playing cricket it quickly became apparent that I couldn't really bowl so, being sporty and athletic, wicketkeeping became an

obvious alternative. Thus it was he would take me off to the St Lawrence ground occasionally to watch Alan Knott keep to Derek Underwood, and with plenty of cricket on terrestrial TV, I could watch him whenever I wanted.

Knott fascinated me from the start. His initials APE were in keeping with his somewhat simian, craggy looks. He stretched constantly, even in the last over of the day, and it always seemed to me this was as much about keeping his mind active and boredom at bay as the limbs loose. Even today I rarely keep wicket (when I do make it on to the field) without a long-sleeved shirt to protect my elbows and there was even a time, when I was much younger, that I had a handkerchief peeping out of my pocket in homage to the great man.

It was Knott who showed me that a fielding side takes its lead from the keeper, that he is their conductor. This was reaffirmed for me when at school I was coached by one of those who just couldn't dislodge him from the England side, the Leicestershire wicketkeeper Roger Tolchard. Watching Knotty I realised that even if you didn't make a run or take a catch you could still play an enormous role in a team's success, even if you couldn't measure that through sheer hard facts. He was always on the move, always the metronome for the team's fielding display.

"The eccentricities of genius", as Dickens called it, shouldn't mask his ability

He brought his own incredible run to an end by agreeing to join Tony Greig in Kerry Packer's World Series experiment. Not only did it offer him some longer-term security, the short-term benefits were evident too – a chance of a more stable family environment in Sydney rather than the nomadic life on the road in England. As a nine-year-old I didn't understand the politics and couldn't work out why he'd voluntarily give up the chance to play for England but by then I'd not only watched him but on one memorable afternoon in Tunbridge Wells he'd coached me too. All I can recall is diving across crash mats in a sports hall and him showing me how to turn your elbow as you landed so that the ball didn't pop out.

If that was exciting, then some 14 years later I kept wicket to the man to whom he was umbilically linked at Kent, Derek Underwood. Playing for a team put together by The Cricketer magazine, I realised after a couple of balls that he really was medium pace and that with his bounce he'd be virtually unplayable on a drying pitch. He'd already had three players caught at silly point when the No. 11 went to cut one and got a faint nick that my gloves somehow closed around. As we walked off, Underwood walked over to me and kindly said, "Alan Knott would have been proud of that catch." I'm sure he was just being very polite but I didn't care. I went straight home and told my father.

Knott got back into the England team at the end of that Ashes series in 1981 and retired after making 70 not out in the last Test at The Oval. His ankle injury and increasing tiredness with touring were major contributing factors. He was certainly individual, "the eccentricities of genius" as Dickens called it, but that shouldn't mask his enormous ability. It's worth remembering that he was replaced by Taylor at first only when he joined Packer's circus and secondly when he retired. He was arguably the last of England's great wicketkeeper-batsmen as opposed to batsmen-wicketkeepers. In the current climate, when the quality of the glovework is seemingly secondary to the ability to score runs, do the former exist any more?

MARK POUGATCH is a journalist and broadcaster for BBC Radio Five Live and BBC Television

ALLAN LAMB
by LAWRENCE BOOTH

The roar of the Lamb

Lawrence Booth admits to an unhealthy obsession
with the man his friends called Limmie

If love is blind, then my relationship with Allan Lamb was more a myopic obsession.
He never knew about it, of course, and the one time I met him I had to fight hard not
to blub pathetically and admit all. I was old enough to know better by then but the two
of us had already been through a lot together.

It had not always been easy. Lamb finished with a Test average of 36.09, which
pained me. His highest Test score was 142, which was frankly careless. And, well, he
was not exactly English, was he? "Limmie," my mates would snigger in a mock-South
African accent, as if that settled the argument. But none of this mattered. Lambie
and I had a bond that transcended trivialities like statistics and passports.

Anyone captivated by Test cricket remembers the series that did it. For me it was
England's trip to the West Indies in 1989–90, which I followed on the radio in my
bedroom, insulated from the world. There was something magical about that faint
crackle and, when Lambie made 132 in England's shock win in the first Test at Sabina
Park, I was under his spell. He later made 119 in Barbados and I can recall the words
of the BBC's Trevor Bailey as another bottom-handed cover-drive – feet in concrete
– propelled the ball to the boundary: "Allan Lamb is a fine player." The emphasis was
on 'is' and 'fine', as if Bailey was reminding us of a truism. At least that is how an
impressionable 14-year-old heard it.

> He was brassy,
> aggressive, irritating –
> and I loved him for it

With Lamb came his adopted county, Northamptonshire – another deeply un-
fashionable choice. (Graham Gooch and Essex would have been so much simpler.)
In 1995, with the help of Anil Kumble, he almost captained us to our first Championship. He was brassy, aggressive, irritating – and I loved him for it. Against
Nottinghamshire we conceded over 500 in the first innings but Lambie insisted on
building a lead rather than declaring behind. He was one of four centurions as

Caribbean king: Lamb, above, reaches his century at Sabina Park against West Indies in 1989–90 and, opposite, flashes a drive during that innings

Northants rattled up 781 for 7 and won by an innings and plenty. I swelled with pride as writers began to refer to us as "the people's choice" (never mind that the people largely ignored county cricket) and nearly wept with frustration when our 12 wins out of 17 were not enough to topple either Warwickshire or Middlesex. We have never come so close since.

By this stage Lambie was long gone as an England player. He had retired from the international game in 1992, which meant that I enjoyed at first hand only the final two-and-a-half years of his imperfect career. Only research could complete the picture. I lapped up tales of his four centuries in the summer of 1984 – three of them against the all-conquering West Indians (he would make six Test hundreds against them in all, my favourite Lambie stat). I rejoiced in the time he hit 18 off Bruce Reid's final over to beat the Aussies in a one-dayer at Sydney. I took vicarious pride in the fact that he had scored a century in only his third Test, against India at The Oval. And I could usually recite his batting average to two decimal places.

Did I regret meeting him? A bit. He would never be the same again

His career post-1990 was, to be honest, a bit of a struggle. But we pulled through. I remember spending a summer holiday in 1990 on a French campsite and waiting anxiously as my brother did the newspaper-and-croissants run. Back he came with the news: Lambie had scored 109 in the second Test against India at Old Trafford. Surely this would silence the carpers, especially after his 139 in the first Test at Lord's (but why did Gooch have to steal the show with that 333?). It was pure solipsism: Lambie existed only to thrill or disappoint me, and I regarded it as a personal triumph when his 142 saved the Wellington Test early in 1992. A few months later I was there at Lord's when Lambie faced what turned out to be his final ball in Test cricket: a grubber from Mushtaq Ahmed that struck him plumb in front. He made 12.

There were three more seasons with Northants and then, just like that, he was gone. There were wranglings over some controversial content in his autobiography; retirement was the only option. But did it have to be so clean and brutal? There was no farewell. Nothing. Those were hard days.

It is virtually impossible to put my finger on why I worshipped Lambie so zealously. He was a hopeless starter and failed far too often for someone who played 79 Tests. He made 14 Test hundreds but only 18 fifties. He could look appalling against spin and tended to push at the ball with those stiff South African wrists. But he had this swagger. He loved to hook and cut and he was short in stature, which is why he scored runs against West Indies. And he had this nerveless, tireless way about him.

When I got the chance to meet him, I could hardly contain myself. Friends of mine had been invited to a day's golf and socialising and the Lambs would be there too. We shook hands and chatted about the ups and downs of Northamptonshire and taking tons off Curtly and Courtney, a subject he knew more about than I did. It was fun but I wondered whether I should have preserved Lambie in the realm of idolatry. Did I regret meeting him? A bit. He would never quite be the same again. But, hell, we would always have Sabina.

LAWRENCE BOOTH writes on cricket for the *Daily Mail* and is the author of several books on cricket

HAROLD LARWOOD
by PETER ROEBUCK

A man undefeated

Having beaten the Australians, Harold Larwood went and joined them. Peter Roebuck profiles one of Engand's greatest fast bowlers, a working man without ego or vanity

Harold Larwood is my favourite cricketer because he was honest, modest, and the epitome of the properly raised working man. Nothing of the celebrity could be found in him, no hint of glamour or touch of tinsel. Harold was a man without pretension or ego, a man sustained by pride in his performance, loyalty to the deserving, and the satisfaction to be taken from the contemplation of a job well done.

He came into the England side as a fast bowler from the mines and left in blood-soaked boots with the Ashes reclaimed. He did the donkey work and the dirty work, and sat back dismissively as his country, or rather its patrician rulers, disowned him. Afterwards, after a long war, he went to Australia, where he was supposed to be hated but was actually understood and admired, and spent the rest of his life there, earning a living in a factory, avoiding the traps and the dazzle and the backslappers, and instead enjoying the simple things: home, family and happy memories.

He knew he had greatness in him

Larwood was born and raised in a mining community near Nottingham, a city of free thinkers from which, in the middle of the previous century, travelling teams of paid cricketers had emerged, professionals who earned their living by playing local teams wherever they went. Nottingham was also a city with a tradition of political radicalism and championing of the working man. Larwood had been born in the right place. He remained independent, believed skill and effort should be rewarded, and retained his beliefs till the last breath left his body.

In some respects Larwood was also born at the right time. Don Bradman was running amok and England was crying out for bowlers. Nothing was worse than losing to those brazen chaps from down under. A cry went out across the land for men with heart and pace, and Larwood and Bill Voce, his mate and fellow miner, were listening.

Unfortunately the pitches between the wars were dopier than a Woodstock hippy. For years Larwood and chums put their backs into their work and watched as modest batsmen met their most ferocious salvos with graceful strokes played on the front foot. It was an affront. Larwood's teeth had been pulled before he had even stepped onto the field. Fast bowlers were turners of sods and hewers of wood, not takers of wickets.

Larwood's spirit rebelled. Between them, Bradman and docile pitches had made him feel tame, unable to do his job. He knew he had greatness in him, and the sort of pace that burns grass, but it remained within, an unexpressed desire. He yearned for a captain with the guts to play a hard game, a physical game, a leader willing to let him mount the sort of bombardment that alone could disturb his opponents. Arthur Carr served the purpose at Nottingham, and few visiting batsmen relished the prospect of playing at Trent Bridge when Harold and Bill were taking the new ball.

For England, though, Larwood was forced to pitch the ball up, aiming at the stumps and never the body. He took numerous floggings but the proud man refused to wilt and kept his thoughts to himself. At last England decided they could take no more and asked Douglas Jardine to take the team to Australia. Although he did not know it, Larwood had found the captain he wanted, a man of unyielding determination, ruthless and committed to victory.

He received an ashtray inscribed "From a grateful captain"

Jardine's strategy, an unrelenting assault directed at the body of the genius, Bradman, allowed no room for error. Extreme pace, stamina and supreme control were required or the plan could not work. Everything depended on Larwood, and it was his finest hour, as he pounded the ball down over after eight-ball over. Defying heat and hard pitches, and driven by the desire to prove his worth and win the Ashes, he terrorised and eventually beat the ageing champions of the antipodes. Spectators howled and batsmen squealed but Jardine and Larwood held firm and, against formidable odds, the Ashes were regained. Not until Bradman was dismisssed for the last time in the series did Jardine allow his injured bowler to leave the field. It must have been a poignant sight, the defeated batsman and the hobbling paceman walking towards the pavilion at the SCG, neither man saying a word.

Attempts were made to tarnish Larwood's reputation with film taken of his action during that epic summer. But only a few deliveries looked ragged, possibly the result of weariness towards the end of a gruelling day. Nevertheless, he did not play for

England again. Jardine did not last much longer either. Although they had scrupulously obeyed the rules of the game, they had ignored those existing mainly in the minds of the romantics. Neither man ever apologised.

Larwood stayed in England, running a sweet shop in Blackpool till Jack Fingleton, an adversary in 1932–33, said he must come back to Australia where a warm welcome awaited. He worked alongside other 'New Australians' and retired in a suburb of Sydney, surrounded by his memories and proudly showing guests an ashtray given by Jardine after the Ashes had been recovered and bearing the inscription "From a grateful captain". He died in his 90s, a man undefeated.

PETER ROEBUCK played for Somerset in the 1970s and 1980s. He is a journalist and author, writing for the *Sydney Morning Herald* among other publications

JOHN LEVER
by ALAN DAVIES

The magical allure of JK

John Lever was a blond who knew how to have fun – and take wickets

How old were you when you first had sporting heroes? Around 10? For me that meant 1976: Barry Sheene, Liam Brady at Highbury, Brendan Foster winning bronze at the Montreal Olympics (resembling an escaped POW needing a pie), plus cricketers from Essex. GA Gooch and KWR Fletcher were too like characters from *The Jungle Book* and *Wind in the Willows* with their bear-ish or rodenty ways. If you were a gentleman who preferred blondes, if you preferred Agnetha to Anni-Frid out of Abba, then there was only one man for you: JK Lever.

JK, better known today as the creator of Harry Potter (under the nom de plume Rowling), first made his name as the finest left-arm fast-medium bowler (but RHB) of his generation. His writing has since overshadowed his cricket but at book signings it is still unmistakeably JK. Blonde hair around the shoulders, curled under and side-parted, with that sardonic smile playing across his lips. Some say a different JK writes the novels, a woman even. Laughable. Ever seen Lever and Rowling in the same room? Harry Potter himself could not pull that off. But this is not the place to discuss his scribbling, rather for cricket nostalgia.

> ## The spectacle of cricket at Southend
> ## in the 70s was too exciting
> ## for this 10-year-old

Alan Knott was an early idol. Having the same name was enough; the Welsh rugby team held a similar appeal as many of them were called Davies. Behind the stumps on television Knott was, as a jealous actor might have it, "in every bloody scene". If not directly involved – a prod to the bowler, a push to mid-off – he would steal the scene with moves approved by aficionados of *Aerobics Oz Style*: bending, squatting and beaming away like an instructor trying to convince you it won't hurt.

My allegiance to Kent, because Knotty played there, was bad form in Essex. Grandad and Dad taught me cricket in the garden while an elder brother attempted to wound me with the stupidly hard ball. Teaching did not stop at forward defensive and bowling over-arm but extended into scoring, which was practised at Woodford

Wells CC. From the boundary, players were named according to headwear, physicality or technique, eg: Black Cap c Baldy b Wrong Foot 12.

We also played, possibly uniquely, 'Dob Cricket'. Take a page of the *Telegraph* (preferably death notices where the print is small) and stick a pin in it. Each 'dob' of the pin represents a ball bowled. Landing on a space means a dot ball. Letters and punctuation marks denote runs, extras or wickets. Sadly the scoring system may now be lost. From memory, 'm' was worth three. Dob cricket was addictive and scorebooks were filled with imaginary games. One holiday on the Isle of Wight the teams were Shanklin and Sandown, who included Clive Lloyd, John Edrich and Brian Luckhurst.

When the time came to sample the county game Essex were using eight different grounds but the best day out was to Southend. Put on a train at Liverpool Street with orders not to lose the elder brother, who wanted to shake me off, my intention was to score diligently. It was easier said than done. The spectacle of cricket at Southend in the 70s was too exciting for this 10-year-old. Down the front you could see huge boundary fielders only feet away. When Keith Boyce threw the ball in, it was a missile. After a four, if you were quick (and rough with smaller boys), you could pick it up to hurl in, leaving a fielder disgruntled as it landed 20 feet behind him when he wanted it lobbed to his hand. All boys try for the middle the first time.

My brother scored throughout, studiously ignoring my quest for the limelight in pursuing the ball, which may explain why one of us became a turn and the other an accountant. Somehow he ate sandwiches at lunch when there were autographs to be sought. Though many were friendly, JK was the star. After another devastating over he trotted towards us. "Good luck in India, John" called someone. Incomprehensible to me, this was noisily endorsed by all. JK turned in modest appreciation. He toured with England that winter taking 10 wickets and a 50 in his first Test – brilliant, heroic, a blond having fun. Things soured later when Bishan Bedi accused him of cheating with a Vaseline strip. JK, according to his autobiography, never forgave him.

Ultimately he played 20 more times for his country and appeared unstoppable for Essex. Rushing in over the wicket like the wind, locks flowing, he took scores of wickets either swinging it in or catching edges. In 1979 JK was one of *Wisden*'s five cricketers of the year. He rocked.

Once we nearly collided as a ball headed towards me at the boundary. As I vaulted a board in anticipation of picking it up, a shouted warning only just prevented me from leaping into the path of JK hurtling round the boundary. At county cricket you could get so close to your heroes it was dangerous.

Perhaps unwittingly JK Lever owes his later career to me. He now coaches at my old school, Bancroft's. The very existence of that school is dependent on my decision not to burn it down on leaving in 1982. Mind you, Hogwarts would probably have him if they ever give up quidditch for a proper game.

ALAN DAVIES is an actor, comedian and supporter of Essex CCC

John Lever

GEOFF MILLER
by ROBERT KITSON

Hooked by the Miller's tale

Robert Kitson reveals his unhealthy obsession with Derbyshire's off-spinning allrounder turned selector and raconteur

Can it really be 25 years ago? Even now I can recite the words of Peter West (that is how distant it was) on the TV highlights: "And there's Geoff Miller, diving for the crease as if he was scoring a rugby try." If you study my treasured video of the epic 1981 NatWest final between Derbyshire and Northamptonshire you will also spot a certain terminally uncool teenager doing an energetic Nobby Stiles-inspired pogo in front of the Lord's pavilion. Those were the days, my friends, when England possessed a bearded spinner who could genuinely bat, bowl and field.

How to explain my perverse attraction to all things 'Dusty' Miller? I have tried before to articulate it in print and succeeded only in painting a picture of deluded youth. My Dad was a Quantocks boy, organically reared on Harold Gimblett and Arthur Wellard. Me? I grew up in a Hampshire village, miles away from the crooked spire of blessed Chesterfield. And yet it was the cricketing men of Derbyshire who burrowed into my soul.

They may have been bottom of the Championship table consistently in the early 1970s but they did have Bob Taylor, whose blue gloves gave him an edge over Alan Knott for us connoisseurs, and an up-and-coming youngster of whom much was expected. This, remember, was late 1973 when Ian Botham had not quite emerged and England were conspicuously short of boy wonders. By the time Viv and Beefy arrived on the scene, it was already far too late.

I christened a rabbit Dusty.
Inevitably it died
within days

And so the madness began. I had a rabbit called Kallicharran but only because I could not say Venkataraghavan. There was a second rabbit too, which I confidently christened Dusty. Inevitably it died within days. I gradually became aware that Derbyshire were not quite the crack professional force I had fondly imagined. As John Wright recalled in his entertaining autobiography, Derbyshire were hardly a

glamour county. When Mike Hendrick broke down they had to carry him off on a door because the club did not have a stretcher.

Around that time the club had a senior official whose nickname was 'Slightly', 'Totally' or 'Absolutely' depending on what time of the day it was. Undeterred, I persuaded Dad to drive me north to see the hallowed turf on which my heroes strode. We stood in silence on the wet outfield at Ilkeston. My blurred picture of Heanor, taken through barbed wire while sitting on Dad's shoulders, remains a classic of the anorak genre.

Soon enough, though, Geoff began to repay my blind faith. He made his England debut at the end of the roasting summer of 1976 and toured each winter with satisfying regularity. Little did either of us know that it would take him until May 1984 to score his maiden first-class century. It was even possible to giggle along with the tongue-in-cheek match reports from India: "When Miller passes 70 an agonising hush descends on the stadium. At 80 stiff drinks are required. At 90 tiles begin to fall from nearby rooftops. At this point the tension starts to get to him . . ."

I dug out my photo of Geoff's car. The word 'stalker' was less commonly used in those days

But he could bat. And bowl. And field. I trekked to Taunton once to see Derbyshire play a one-day game. Before my disbelieving eyes Botham hit Miller for five successive fours en route to a blistering hundred. When Derbyshire batted, Geoff did exactly the same to Both and finished unbeaten on 80-odd in a perfectly paced run chase.

Jim Laker once described a late cut of his in a televised game at Chesterfield as reminiscent of Peter May. And then there was his famous catch from Chris Tavaré's juggled deflection which won England the Melbourne Test in 1982–83. Back at home I celebrated by digging out my photo of Geoff's sponsored car, taken surreptitiously in the Southampton car park. The word 'stalker' was less commonly used in those days.

Adulthood hits us all eventually. I ventured shyly into sportswriting and found myself required to phone Geoff, by now with Essex, for a couple of bland quotes to publicise the forthcoming weekend's Sunday league fixtures. It did not make for Pulitzer Prize-winning stuff. Me: "Er, how's life in Essex?" Geoff: "I'm living in digs in Braintree." Me: "Oh. Are the pitches turning any more than at Derby?" Geoff: "Pigs might fly." I gently replaced the receiver and sat there in stunned silence, waist-deep in shattered illusions.

It could all have ended there. I could have thrown away the yellowing cuttings, the benefit tie, the lookalike wristbands and the Dusty videos. By the time he retired Geoff's record was not as good as either of us would have liked. Thirty-four Tests, in which he averaged 25.80 with the bat and took 60 wickets at 30.98, does not merit obvious hero worship. The confidence to match his talent was not always evident and a bad back – the result of a car crash as a teenager – did not help.

But then word arrived that Geoff was carving out an alternative career as one of the funniest after-dinner speakers on the circuit, his self-deprecating act based around his own mediocrity as a cricketer. For reasons I still cannot entirely comprehend, he has also become an England selector. Duncan Fletcher and Michael Vaughan may have helped mastermind England's Ashes success last year but I think we all know who was really behind it.

This season, of course, Geoff and David Graveney have allegedly been the wise men behind the successful elevation of Monty Panesar and Chris Read. If true, it is another feather in Geoff's multi-dimensional cap and fresh justification for those of us who still pluck at the hem of the great man's garment. Growing old alongside a schoolboy hero can be depressing. Thirty-three years on, Geoff still makes me smile.

ROBERT KITSON is rugby union correspondent of *The Guardian*

JIM PARKS
by MICHAEL SIMKINS

Sunny Jim

Michael Simkins on the only man who could drag him from the sweetshop

The actor Tom Courtenay once glumly remarked to me as he scanned the football results for his beloved Hull City, "You don't choose the team you support . . . It chooses you."

I already knew. I grew up in a sweetshop on the south coast, a short bus ride from the home of Sussex County Cricket Club, and from the first time I saw them, as a 10-year-old boy in 1967, I was hooked. The team I had stumbled on was like my favourite chocolate bar (which at the time was Macintosh's Caramac): packed with good things but likely to raise your blood pressure if you indulged yourself for too long. And the batsman who could most quickly send my sugar level soaring was Jim Parks.

Crinkly-haired, sun-tanned, his face permanently creased into a broad smile, he seemed the embodiment of Sussex. He was already a star of the side. He had played for the county for 18 years and was just finishing a Test career as England's wicketkeeper-batsman.

As it happened my first glimpse of him in that summer of '67 coincided with a particularly unhappy stint as Sussex captain. But the nation's loss was my gain: after giving up the international gloves to Alan Knott and the domestic captaincy to Mike Griffith his form returned. He barely missed a county match for the next five years and I was there to witness most of them.

Parks was, of course, a fine keeper but it was his wonderful batting that attracted me. In a fragile post-Dexter batting order the accepted wisdom among the stripy deckchairs and wheeling seagulls at Hove was that as long as Parks was still at the crease hope sprung eternal. It is a motto I still believe in today.

A batsman of stinging drives and jaunty footwork, he seemed to play the game as it should be played, with total commitment yet without a hint of malice or pretension. Although a destructive one-day player, he always seemed to be enjoying himself whatever the occasion. I always imagined he was the sort of bloke who carried a bag of Fox's Glacier Mints in his pocket.

For the next five years Jim Parks was my hero. I collected his autograph so many times that he must have thought I was learning to forge his signature, and his autobiography, the unfortunately titled *Runs in the Sun* (my mum always said it sounded like something you'd pick up on holiday), was the most cherished of my burgeoning collection of second-hand cricket books, especially when I discovered a letter sent from the author to the previous owner of the tome nestling among its pages.

In 1970 I watched in mute supplication as he stood alone against the might of Lancashire in the Gillette Cup final (my first trip up to the home of cricket and one which provided my first pre-pubescent experience of heartbreak). At Eastbourne the same year I saw him strike a sublime and effortless 150 against Essex, bringing up his hundred by driving the ball straight into my sandwiches on the boundary edge at deep extra cover. But mostly my memories are a patchwork of wonderful 40s or 50s, usually seen after tea when I could escape from school, often with Sussex up against it and always in even time.

It took the sharp eyes of my dad, accompanying me to a John Player League match while on a rare break from sweetshop duties, to spot that Parks, while batting, performed an intricate and involved ritual of bat-twirling and box-tugging before each ball, finishing always with him transferring the bat from right to left hand and sweeping it momentarily across the return crease before settling down for the next delivery. I tried copying this talismanic ceremony for myself in school cricket until told to "bloody well stop arseing about" by my games master.

When Parks was summarily dispensed with at the end of 1972, much of the sparkle went out of cricket at Hove and when, the following season, I saw him keeping wicket for Somerset it was a surreal and disturbing image, a bit like discovering your dad dressed in women's clothing. It was typical of Parks that he forgot and forgave, eventually returning to the club as marketing manager and later president.

Nowadays the feisty, up- and-at-'em team spawned by the Moores-Adams dynasty seems a far cry from the sunny unpredictability of four decades ago. Nonetheless I was at Hove along with 3,500 other disbelieving souls to watch their first Championship pennant unfurled in 2003. As Murray Goodwin pulled the ball to the boundary to bring up the bonus point that sealed the club's first Championship, I glimpsed Parks sitting quietly on the railing of a staircase at the side of the pavilion enjoying the celebrations. Alone, unnoticed, his smile was as broad as ever.

And then, earlier this season, while strolling round the boundary at Arundel I finally met the man. I was too dazzled and tongue-tied to ask him about his batting ritual or whether he had indeed a penchant for Glacier Mints: but it was something special. As an actor of nearly 30 years standing I've met and chatted with some of the greats: Tom Courtenay, of course, Ian McKellen, Anthony Perkins, Lauren Bacall, even Benny and Bjorn from Abba. But I tell you: none of them comes close.

MICHAEL SIMKINS is an actor, usually seen on TV playing experts or unsuspecting husbands and author of the highly-acclaimed *Fatty Batter: Or how cricket saved my life, then ruined it*

GRAEME POLLOCK
by SIMON KUPER

All the time in the world

Pollock's ease with his batting and family life was cherished by Simon Kuper

When I close my eyes and think back to the Wanderers, Transvaal are batting and I am queuing for an ice cream behind the stand. The man in front of me, a little bearded white guy, is throwing a temper tantrum at the black ice-cream seller, whom he accuses of being slow. "You're so stupid," the bearded man shouts, with dirty words thrown in. "You should not have this job. Quickly give me change." He enunciates every syllable, the way some white South Africans do. Even as a 10-year-old I can see he is expressing frustrations that come from somewhere else. The black man is silently getting the ice-cream and the change because he is not allowed to say anything back. As a child I am not either. Today I wonder where those two men are now.

In those days – the late 1970s and early 1980s – we used to stay with my grandparents in northern Johannesburg during the Christmas holidays. We were refugees from frozen Europe. At home in Holland the week before I would have cycled through the darkness into the west wind to school. In Johannesburg I would toddle off in mid-morning with my green scorebook for a day at the Wanderers. It was only 15 minutes' walk around the corner and I often went by myself.

> ## His Test average of 60.97 is the highest in history after Bradman's

Inside the ground everyone is white except for one small stand full of blacks. It is the holidays and the crowd is happy. When a pretty girl walks down our terrace towards the exit, the stand accompanies her with a concert of wolf-whistles. The Transvaal has some of the world's best players, men like Clive Rice, Jimmy Cook and, of course, Graeme Pollock. Life is good in South Africa.

Pollock is at the crease. People put down their newspapers when he is batting. He is already a legend, his future behind him: he played his last Test match for South Africa as a 26-year-old in 1970, after which the country was banned from international cricket because of apartheid. His Test average of 60.97 is the highest in history after Don Bradman's. Though the man I am watching still hopes to play Test cricket

Second to Bradman: Pollock during his 125 for South Africa against at Trent Bridge in 1965

again, he never will. We at the Wanderers are among the select few who will ever see him bat.

Most white South Africans I meet consider this an outrage. Among them cricket is a daily topic of conversation, not the private perversion I feel it is in England and Holland. Even my aunts offer regular updates on the score at the Wanderers.

The wicket is baked and fast. The bowler – perhaps it is Robin Jackman of Rhodesia – drops the ball just short. When Pollock is batting, you get a wonderful sense of where the ball is landing, because he is already in position waiting for it. Watching him taught me that the difference between the great athletes and the rest of us is the time they have. This is true of Wayne Rooney in football or Jason Kidd in basketball: they see everything early. The only batsman I ever saw who picked up the ball as quickly as Pollock was David Gower. I remember Gower once shaping to play a backward defensive against Malcolm Marshall, and then, hearing the cry of no-ball, trying to hook him.

Unlike Richards, Pollock never turns pro in England so never falls out of love with cricket

But Pollock's technique is better than Gower's. When the South African cover drives he does not flap at the ball while falling away. He stands up almost to his full regal height, lifts his bat straight back and thumps the short ball through the covers. The only batsman I have seen hit the ball as hard at the Wanderers is tiny Alvin Kallicharran, opening for Orange Free State, who proves that it is all about timing.

Pollock could thump the ball through the covers all day. Sometimes he does. It is not just that he is a genius. Unlike the sportsmen I revere in Europe, he is also an ordinary bloke. As far as I can understand, he has a regular office job in Johannesburg. Cricket is his hobby. It is the same for most of his team-mates: they are part of normal white daily life. Cook is my second cousin's schoolteacher. Ali Bacher is the husband of one of my distant cousins. Xenophon Balaskas, a Springbok of the 1930s and possibly the best Greek cricketer ever, is a pal of my grandfather who gives me some nets at his house. Pollock's old team-mate Barry Richards shows up as coach of one of our local cricket clubs in Holland. He umpires a kids' match in which I take two slip catches and score seven runs, my team's highest score. Richards says something nice about me. My father invites him round to dinner as a fellow South African. Richards comes round that same evening but by then I have caught chickenpox and cannot go downstairs.

Unlike Richards, Pollock never turns pro in England. He, therefore, never falls out of love with cricket. He seems content to play out a largely unwitnessed career. He does not say much about apartheid but, according to my more liberal relatives, he is known to disapprove of it. Recently he told this magazine: "We could have made a bigger noise about apartheid at the time – I think that's a genuine criticism. In hindsight perhaps we should have done more."

There was a simplicity to the man: to his haircuts, to his batting and to the things he thought and said. It was appropriate that he and his brother Peter and his nephew Shaun and his sons Anthony and Andrew, who both played for a while, had such ordinary names. The Pollocks were not stars. They just happened to be excellent cricketers and one of them was rather more than that.

SIMON KUPER is the author of *Football Against the Enemy*. He grew up mostly in the Netherlands but his family origins are in South Africa

MIKE PROCTER
by JOHN INVERDALE

The inimitable man

**As Mike Procter bowled fast off the wrong foot John Inverdale
was doing himself an injury trying to copy him**

There are probably a lot of men in their forties and fifties walking around the country
these days with bad postural problems and inflamed tendons, all because of Mike
Procter.

If you were a schoolboy in Gloucestershire during the 1970s, and you were interested in cricket, you wanted to be Mike Procter. No disrespect to Zaheer Abbas or
Sadiq Mohammad or any of the other local boys but Gloucestershire was called
Proctershire with good reason. He was as talismanic a figure as you could get with
bat and ball and the best thing about him was he bowled in such a ridiculous way
– front on, off the wrong foot and fast, really fast.

Which is probably why so many of us are permanently damaged; it was a lot more
interesting going into the nets at school and trying to bowl like Proccy even if it
meant you fell over half the time and every other ball was a full toss. And how much
fun was it trying to work out the run-up with one extra or one fewer pace, so that
you came crashing down on the wrong foot?

> **It was the most exciting
> thing I've seen on
> a cricket field**

There must be orthopaedic surgeons the length and breadth of the land who have
made money out of Procter-impersonators. But one day above all stands out – never
to be forgotten for two reasons. I was thoroughly mature by this time, and more
interested in girls, music and drink at university in Southampton than perfecting my
Procter run-up when Gloucestershire played Hampshire in the semi-finals of the 1977
Benson and Hedges Cup. The Sex Pistols were singing 'God Save the Queen' but there
were not too many punks with safety pins through their noses and chess-board hair
of orange and green inside the county ground for the game.

Barry Richards and Procter – the two great South Africans isolated by apartheid
– were in direct opposition. Gordon Greenidge was there too. Is it a sign of age that

just by mentioning their names you are transported back to another time and the hairs really do bristle on the back of your neck?

If you are of that vintage, you will know what happened. Procter took four wickets in five balls including a hat-trick. It was probably the most exciting thing I've ever seen on a cricket field or at least partly saw because the summer of '77 was a proper summer and, while not as warm as the previous two, it provided a pollen fiesta. Until that semi-final I had no idea I suffered from hay fever but, as the day progressed and the pollen did whatever pollen does, I started sneezing relentlessly and irritatingly for those surrounding me in the stand. There are only so many times you can apologise and mid-way through Procter's demolition of the Hampshire line-up I was forced to bale out of my seat and position myself behind the stand, allowing the crowd to tell me what was going on.

Since that afternoon I have never been to a cricket match without the necessary medication but on that particular day the pollen did to me what Proccy did to Hampshire.

So long as we never meet, he will be forever young

Given the job that I have been lucky enough to do now for nearly 25 years, it is perhaps one of those strange quirks of fate that I have never met him, and in a funny way I do not want to. Mike Procter will always be to me the tousle-haired blond bombshell flying in to deliver unplayable deliveries – not an ICC official as he now is.

I read a great deal about the criticism he received for imposing the three-match ban on Harbhajan Singh during the series against Australia and got progressively more cross. I mused about redressing the balance in my column in the *Daily Telegraph*. And then I wondered why I was getting so aggravated and I realised it was because one of my teenage heroes was being lampooned so unfairly.

Perhaps those kind of irrational loyalties are best left in their own time and space. This was indeed the summer of John Lydon and the Silver Jubilee and, if the iPod had been invented, mine would have played Fleetwood Mac's 'Rumours' every hour of every day. But it was also the summer that Mike Procter did for me what Botham did for others in '81 and Andrew Flintoff for the new power generation in 2005. For that he remains one of those figures that defines a period of my life. And so long as we never meet, he will be forever young.

JOHN INVERDALE is a BBC sports broadcaster and journalist

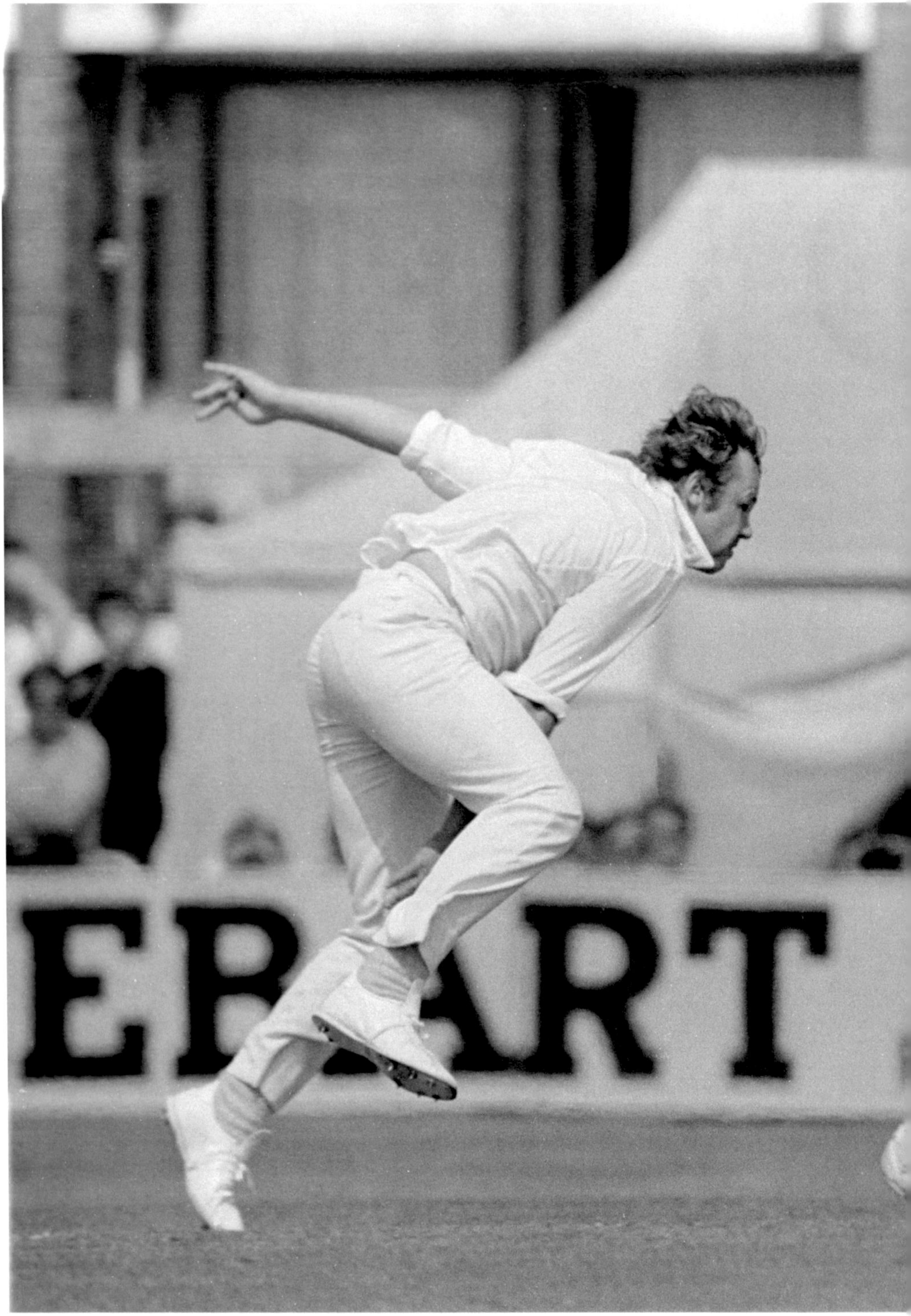

Demolition: Procter bowling for Gloucestershire against Hampshire in the 1977 B&H
semi-final. Barry Richards is the non-striker

CLIVE RADLEY
by DJ TAYLOR

Who said only turkeys come out of Norfolk?

Amid the lashing rain and flat plains of a Norfolk childhood DJ Taylor relished the exploits of a local hero

I turned up the autograph album only the other day. Begun in 1972 and abandoned a year later but, given the constraints of milieu – ie; a compiler who rarely set foot outside sequestered Norfolk – impressive in its scope. The ex-England football captain Billy Wright is there, tapped by my father on a League Cup final trip to Wembley, and Brian Clough – old Big 'Ead proving a lot more amenable to pre-teen stalkers than portly Geoff Hurst. Pride of place, though, belongs to a single, lavender-tinted page towards the front of the book. Here, bunched together – they were all garnered on the same afternoon, possibly even in the same couple of minutes – lie the signatures of three England internationals: Peter Parfitt, Bill Edrich and Clive Radley. In fact Radley has written what looks like 'Clive Gatling', or maybe 'Clive Glazebrook'. It didn't matter. The man signed. I was there.

> ### He was a nudger, a steerer, a clubber, a rooter-about in the rough

The occasion was a charity match somewhere out on the Norfolk flat, in the late summer of 1972, between an Edrich Family XI and a Lord's Taverners select that included, as well as some serious cricketers, such luminaries of stage and screen as Roy Hudd and Dad's Army's Ian Lavender. The serious cricket and the celebrity slapstick alternated from one over to the next, and devious manipulation ensured a 272-run tie. Radley, inevitably, was out first ball, scooping a good-length delivery into the arms of a grateful mid-on. At least I got to speak to him. "I go to your old school, Mr Radley", I announced in my 12-year-old's quaver. "Who's your form-master?" the great man affably lobbed back. "I don't know. We've got a new one coming in the autumn," I returned. And that was that.

For about six or seven years, all through the clamorous 1970s, Clive Radley was my cricketing hero. The reason for this 7.45am swoop on the sports pages of the *Telegraph* every day between May and September to check the Middlesex score was

simple local patriotism. Radley was an Old Norvicensian, the only former Norwich School boy, so far as I knew, to make any kind of fist of professional sport. Testimonies to his early prowess lay everywhere. Mr Ninham, the French master, had played in the same 1st XI as him and remembered his practice sessions: setting up a wicket at one end of the playground at the start of the lunchbreak and retiring from it, undefeated, half an hour later. Every day. Lounging in the library, as dense Norfolk rain beat upon the window, I sometimes used to look up accounts of school games played in the late 1950s: a meaty demonstration of just how prodigious teenage cricket prodigies can be. He was an allrounder in those days, bowling twisty leg-breaks, and a specimen match report might run: Norwich School 202–3 declared (Radley 147 no), Gresham's 58 (Radley 7–20) . . .

As a teenage cricket fan, I subscribed to the Corinthian ideal. Boycott was a dour northern clogger. My opinion of Ian Botham I took from my father – "a yob . . . but you'd like to have him in your team." I favoured gentlemanly tacticians like Mike Brearley, elegant ex-public schoolboys who swayed into the ball as it rose and got by on deft square cuts and effortless glances. Curiously, Radley's style was light-years away from these I Zingari-sanctioned exemplars.

He was a nudger, a steerer, a clubber, a rooter-about in the rough, a scamper-down-the-pitch merchant. He was also, at least in the period when I took an interest in him, probably the best occupant of the first-wicket-down spot in English cricket. Each September, as the home Test series ground to a close, when the pundits of *Test Match Special* chewed over likely additions to the winter touring squad, Brian Johnston or EW Swanton would suavely opine that surely it was time for the name of CT Radley to be added to the upper order.

Even in my mid-20s I turned to the sports pages to ensure that reliable Clive was doing the business

Somehow it never was. He made the Test squad in 1977–78, at the advanced age of 33, quite by chance – drafted in from a nearby coaching appointment when Mike Brearley broke his arm in Pakistan. My father instantly composed a letter to the local paper asking them (superfluously) to confirm that this was the first O.N. call-up in history. Memory insists that he was a fixture for the next couple of years, but alas the stats confirm a bare eight Test appearances (average 48, high-point an eight-hour 158 in his second Test against New Zealand) until Rodney Hogg hit him on the head in a warm-up game on the following winter's tour and put him out of international cricket for ever.

Domestically, though, there was another decade to come. The career-best 200 against Northants was struck as late as 1985. Even in my mid-20s, with the Middlesex XI full of upstart youngsters one had never heard of, I still made a point of turning to the sports pages to ensure that reliable Clive was doing the business. Not long back I found a picture of his 60-something figure at the crease on the Middlesex website: grey-haired, stouter, but not in the least gone to seed. It produced the same sensation as the sight of Martin Peters, brought out on to the pitch at Carrow Road a month or two back to preside over the lottery draw: one of those titanic ghosts from childhood, a molten god forever rampaging over the endless greensward, next to whom a file of debased modern descendants can only finick and fret.

DJ TAYLOR is a novelist and critic and former ornament of the Captain Scott Invitation XI, where his career batting average was a modest 5

DEREK RANDALL
by MARCUS BERKMANN

By royal appointment

The restless Randall was often overlooked and
undervalued but not by **Marcus Berkmann**

Cricket, as we all know, is a team game played by individuals and no cricketer can have
been more beguilingly individual than Derek Randall. Modest of stature, equipped
with a pixieish demeanour and liable to doff his cap at insane Australian fast bowlers,
Randall was a one-off. Viewed with the dispassionate gaze of hindsight, his figures may
not look much: 47 Tests between 1976–77 and 1984, 79 innings, 2,470 runs, with seven
hundreds and 12 fifties, five not outs, average 33.37.

After Randall was dropped for the last time the role of Slightly Frustrating Under-
achieving England Middle Order Batsman was occupied by Allan Lamb, Mike Gatting,
Graeme Hick, Mark Ramprakash and John Crawley, each of whom drove me mad at
various times in their own way. But Randall I forgave everything.

Although 47 Tests is not a bad haul for a top-six batsman who did not score a
huge number of runs, I felt at the time that he should have played more and I feel it
still. Randall was, for me, the most ill-used and underestimated batsman of his era,
allowed fewer chances than his contemporaries, and punished more swiftly for every
failure. Writing these words, I feel my teeth starting to grind uncontrollably.

He is, of course, best known for the Centenary Test of 1976–77. It was only his
fifth Test but, if you are going to score an epic 174 against Australia, this was the Test
to do it in. Mere months before Kerry Packer turned the game upside down and
inside out, this was a grand celebration of all that had gone before, without the
slightest clue of what was to come.

The Queen was there, so were thousands of elderly former cricketers, and Randall
produced the performance of the game. England needed 463 runs to win and astound-
ingly came within 46 runs of it.

The cap-doffing incident followed a particularly well-directed Dennis Lillee
bouncer. There could be no better way to disarm the old growler. Another bouncer
was flat-batted to the mid-wicket boundary "with a speed and power that made many
a rheumy eye turn to the master of the stroke, the watching Sir Donald Bradman.
Words cannot recapture the joy of that moment." This was Wisden's unusually effusive
description. It was my hero's defining innings and, needless to say, I did not see a
ball of it.

Later games, though, I remember with unnatural clarity. Randall was always a
nervous starter. At times, when he was out of form, he could look as though he had

never actually batted before and had just wandered on to the pitch by mistake. We who revered him sat through these occasions in torment, hoping he would somehow survive his first few overs, for when he finally found his touch everything clicked in the most magnificent way.

He had that ability, most recently seen in Kevin Pietersen (who otherwise resembles him in no way at all) to play shots you did not think were possible and make them look easy. It was an outrageous talent that communicated the sheer joy of batting. For Randall Test cricket never seemed like just another day at the office. He played the game as we thought we would if we were in his shoes, only with 2,000 times more natural ability.

True, his game was not without its technical flaws. Like so many Test batsmen he had a tendency to nibble fatally outside off stump. Apparently the man himself believed that his relatively short reach made him vulnerable to such balls, although his reach never seemed that short when he was swooping on balls in the covers like a hyperactive orang-utan.

Low centre of gravity, long arms, astounding instincts: what else do you need? The fielding, of course, was his great extra value to a side. It was said, so often that I probably said it in my sleep, that he was worth an extra 20 runs to his side in the field, although I remember once arguing in the pub that it should be 23, while someone else said 18. Those who did not buy into Randall really did not buy into him. Their number included several England selectors.

But, though constantly shoved up and down the order, Randall had a tendency to score runs when they mattered. I particularly remember a gritty and ground-out 105 at Edgbaston against Pakistan in 1982 when he was opening the batting, mainly because no one else would. At Melbourne he batted at No. 3 but I always thought he looked more comfortable at Nos. 6 or 7, at which positions he averaged in the mid-40s.

My favourite innings of his, better than any of the hundreds, was an 83 at Trent Bridge against New Zealand in 1983. Coming in at 169 for 5, he and Ian Botham flayed the Kiwi bowling to all corners. Botham bludgeoned a century and stole the headlines but it was Randall's batting that delighted the connoisseurs. In one over from Richard Hadlee, a Nottinghamshire team-mate who at the time was taking wickets pretty much when he felt like it, Randall hit three boundaries in three balls through the off side. Each ball was slightly different, each shot was slightly different and the result was the same. It was joyous and sublime.

The next year Randall got 0 and 1 against West Indies and was dropped forever. Typically he had his most productive county season in 1985, when England were trouncing Australia and no middle-order places were available. It was not always a lucky career but it was an honourable and at times brilliant one. Someone put the Centenary Test on DVD, please, and add that Hadlee over if there is room.

MARCUS BERKMANN is the author of three books on cricket, *Rain Men, Zimmer Men* and *Ashes to Ashes*

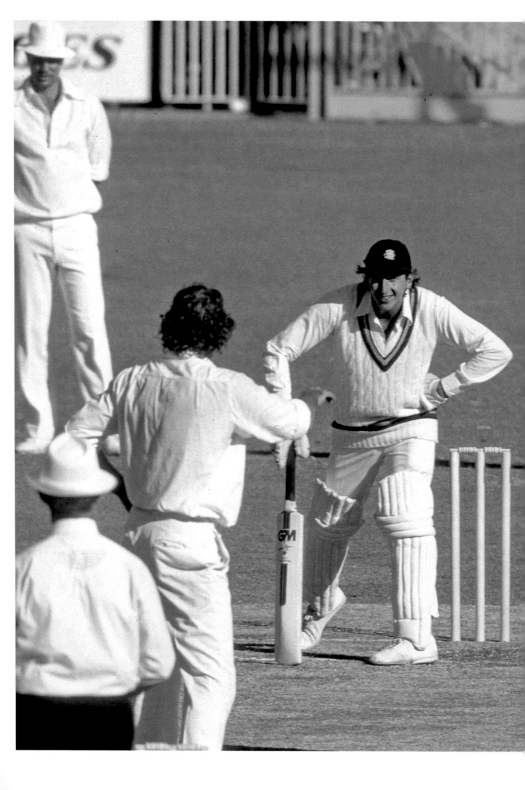

Disarming: Randall stares down Dennis Lillee in the Centenary Test of 1976–77 at Melbourne

JOHN REID
by DES WILSON

Star of the backwoods

John Reid spent weekdays selling fuel to farmers, weekends batting in the local park and holidays playing for New Zealand. Des Wilson celebrates a remarkable allrounder

Oamaru on the South Island of New Zealand is base camp for a farming community. Fifty years back it had no pubs; the sale of alcohol was prohibited. You "dined out" at the local pie cart. There was an "opera house", a milk bar and a weekly dance. There were four cricket clubs, none of them able to guarantee 11 players every Saturday afternoon. And there was John Reid, who, had he played for one of the Ashes countries, would now be a cricket legend.

After Shell appointed Reid its local manager the New Zealand captain could have chosen to drive to the nearest city to play more appropriately competitive cricket. Instead he joined the weakest of the Oamaru clubs. He practised on an uneven concrete wicket at the local park and on Saturdays faced players unable to challenge the power of his batting or the pace of his bowling.

To appreciate Reid's achievement you have to imagine Ian Botham with no county to play for, only the village team on a Saturday; Botham unpaid and with no commercial contracts, with no proper practice wickets and minimal first-class cricket, much of that mediocre; Botham combining the captaincy of his country with running a local Shell depot and, finally, having no world-class team-mates to share the burden of his country's reputation.

> He was an aggressive
> allrounder who made
> things happen

For years Reid alone stood between New Zealand and humiliation. Neville Cardus called him "a club cricketer in excelsis" and that is what he was: a club cricketer who from time to time slipped away to do what club cricketers dream of.

His greatness is not fully reflected by the statistics, impressive as they are. He averaged over 40 in 246 first-class games, most of them for the national side, and took 466 wickets at 22.60; he also played 58 Tests, averaging 33 and taking 85 wickets. What

those figures conceal is how many momentous performances were produced in desperate circumstances or when Reid was virtually without support. In 1951, for instance, he scored a century for Wellington while the remaining 10 players contributed 39.

Like Botham (and Keith Miller), Reid habitually scored runs when they were most needed and took wickets or a blinding catch at just the right time. He was that kind of cricketer – an aggressive allrounder who made things happen. The best of all New Zealand cricket writers, RT Brittenden, wrote that Reid was "never more dangerous than when his back was to the wall . . . he breathed life into a game by his very presence".

Shortly after Reid came to Oamaru I was one of a handful who gathered on a Saturday morning to bowl at him so that he could prepare for New Zealand's 1955–56 tour of India and Pakistan. As he politely and sensitively patted back this 14-year-old's innocuous slow medium-pacers he must have wondered how on earth this could be described as "preparing". Yet in the first match of that tour, in Karachi, coming from the chill of a South Island winter to steamy heat, he took for 7 for 28 and scored 150 not out. It was a difficult tour, yet in first-class games Reid hit 1,032 runs, averaging more than 50, and took 39 wickets.

The following season, while still in Oamaru, he led New Zealand to their first Test victory – over West Indies at Auckland. That ended 26 winless and painful years, in which they played 44 Tests. What a moment for Kiwi cricket.

Reid performed well on his first two England tours. He was 20 when chosen to tour as reserve wicketkeeper in 1949, but he scored nearly 1,500 runs and forced his way into the Test team, where he thrived. He scored another 1,500 on the 1958 tour. But Reid's best performances were reserved for South Africa, in 1961–62, when he led his side to two Test wins, hit seven tour centuries in nine innings and scored more Test runs than any two of his colleagues.

Thank God that John Reid was a New Zealander

Sprinkled throughout that time there were some memorable Plunket Shield moments. At a time when officials elsewhere in the world were pushing for "brighter cricket" Reid was a one-man sunbeam, with the best moment of all a stunning 296 for Wellington in 1962–63 – with 15 sixes, a world record until 1995.

For 10 years he carried the weight of leading a sub-standard Test team. When he eventually retired he had appeared in 58 of New Zealand's 86 Tests and led them in 36. His acceptance without complaint of the burdens thrust upon him, his modesty, his courage and his skill built the foundations that Hadlee, Crowe, Turner and others were later to build on.

Now in his 70s, having been for a while a respected international referee, Reid lives quietly on the North Island. Does he ever wonder what he could have achieved at a different time or in a different place? The answer must be much more. But thank God for New Zealand cricket that John Reid was a New Zealander.

One last memory of Reid: as he walked without celebrity down the main street of Oamaru, a 14-year-old approached him with a piece of paper containing his "selection" for the New Zealand team for an upcoming Test. Reid solemnly studied it and made one or two comments, before assuring the boy his suggestions would be fully considered by him and the other selectors. I have never forgotten the thrill of that moment. And I will never forget John Reid.

DES WILSON is a journalist and author who has also worked for the England and Wales Cricket Board, been chairman of Friends of the Earth and president of the Liberal Party

BARRY RICHARDS
by GAVYN DAVIES

The caged eagle

Apartheid cost Barry Richards a proper Test career and a shot at greatness.
Gavyn Davies on the mightiest might-have-been.

Some cricketers fulfil their talent. Others waste it. And a very few have it wasted for
them. Barry Richards, a man of prodigious ability, was never given the chance to prove
he was one of the greatest batsmen ever. Yet that he was.

I first saw him bat on a cold Southampton morning in May 1968. Batting at No. 4
against Glamorgan, he was undone by the off-cutters of Don Shepherd in both innings,
scoring four runs in the match. Hampshire fans wondered whether the golden-haired
and athletic South African, who seemed to carry his own sunshine around with him,
could adjust to the greyness of an English summer. We need not have worried. In a
wet and miserable season the 22-year-old was soon asked to open the innings and
he responded with 2,395 first-class runs at 47. He finished second behind Geoff
Boycott in the national averages and was made one of *Wisden*'s Five Cricketers of
the Year.

> All great batsmen have
> time to play shots.
> Richards had aeons

His reputation in South African club cricket had been cemented when he played
an innings with the leading edge of his bat because it was too easy for him with the
full face, a feat he briefly repeated in county cricket. A heavy scorer for Natal, he
should have won Test caps during the Australian tour of South Africa in 1966–67
but the Springboks had a greater embarrassment of riches than at any time before or
since. After a short stay at Gloucestershire, who preferred to hire Mike Procter, he
moved to Hampshire in 1968 still unproven.

Not for long. In his early years his batting was founded on a flawless defensive
technique, influenced by pictures of Sir Leonard Hutton hanging on the walls at
Durban High School, and on cover-driving so perfect that it was soon compared
favourably with that of Wally Hammond. His drives were a combination of exqui-
site timing and flowing arms. He never seemed to hit the ball hard but unerringly

found the gaps, the ball seeming to accelerate as it sped to the fence. When bowlers learnt that he was rather good off the front foot they started to drop it short, only to find his square and late cutting were a match for his driving. Over time his leg-side play also developed strongly and the on-drive past midwicket's left hand became a staple.

All great batsmen have time to play shots. Richards had aeons. His footwork was uncanny and he often appeared in place before the ball left the bowler's hand. He once said it amused him to decide where to hit the ball before it was bowled and at the time his ability to hit any delivery to any part of the ground was unique. He may not have had Kevin Pietersen's raw power but he had the same ability to flick his wrists at the last moment, guiding the ball in unexpected directions. And, when in the mood, Richards was much harder to get out.

So this was the batsman who stepped forward to face a strong Australian team at Cape Town in January 1970. Grounds were packed that year, with many of the country's non-whites supporting the Australians for political reasons. Two scores of around 30 contributed to a Springbok win in a low-scoring opening match. Moving on to Durban, his home town, he scored his maiden Test century in 116 balls; the only false stroke in his 140 was the last. He and Graeme Pollock, the two pre-eminent talents of their generation, added 103 runs in an hour after lunch and Pollock's 274 paved the way for an innings win. Many called it the best partnership in a generation. More big scores, including another century, followed for Richards as South Africa completed a clean sweep. He averaged 72 in the series and a decade at the pinnacle of international cricket surely awaited.

Yet Richards and Pollock never batted together again at Test level. Their country was rightly banned from Test cricket over its apartheid policies, which Richards, to his great credit, demonstrated against. There was occasional talk of him qualifying for England but instead he faced years of frustration on the county and Currie Cup circuits.

Bradman said he was
the best right-handed
opener who ever lived

At that level Richards was far, far too good. He scored runs at will and sometimes with an air of arrogant ill humour. Nine centuries before lunch and a career average of 54 merely hinted at his untapped ability. A better measure, perhaps, was his unbeaten 325 for South Australia in a single day at Perth, batting against Dennis Lillee, Graham McKenzie and Tony Lock. There were times when only one man could get him out – himself.

There were high spots as he meandered through a decade of county cricket. Hampshire won the Championship in 1973 and Richards averaged 51, providing with Gordon Greenidge the best opening partnership in world cricket at the time. Greenidge would go on to enjoy a great Test career but no one who watched Hampshire had any doubt about which of the two had the supreme natural gift.

Don Bradman did not lavish much praise on lesser mortals but even he was impressed by Barry Richards. Bradman called him the best right-handed opener who ever lived and chose him in his all-time XI. That is good enough for me.

GAVYN DAVIES is a former government economics adviser and was BBC chairman from 2001–04. He has since co-founded an independent asset management company

GARRY SOBERS
by DUNCAN HAMILTON

Love at first sight

**The game was almost too easy for Garry Sobers, remembers
Duncan Hamilton, who fell for the great man at Trent Bridge**

He came through the pavilion gate like the Great Gatsby gliding into a black-tie ball.
There was a swaggering elegance about this entrance. I registered it in the way he lifted
his patrician gaze towards the summer sky and the aristocratic entitlement inherent in
every stride of his walk.

Suddenly he paused with a stage-professional's timing – meretriciously readjusting
his gloves and shifting the bat beneath his left arm – so he lingered in his own light
and we could see him more clearly in its brightness.

With his upturned collar and a long-sleeved shirt loosely buttoned at the cuffs,
he was the epitome of style and starry glamour. He had an insouciance that simultaneously inspired worship and envy. And when he reached the crease, I remember
he took guard in his own good time; no one had the temerity to rush him. He glanced
around with exaggerated care, as if the placing of the field mattered. But, of course,
it didn't. It was an act, another piece of thespian showboating.

For it struck me in retrospect that it was never a question of how many runs Garry
Sobers could score. It was a matter of how many he wanted to score that day against
Lancashire in late August 1970.

> ### He hit a six that rose not
> ### more than four feet. It would
> ### have killed a whale

The scorecard tells me that Sobers made 52. I did not care then and do not care
now about the statistics of the innings. What captivated me were the aesthetics of it.
Divine sparks flew from his bat.

Sobers demonstrated a savage grace that on the one hand verged on the vengeful,
as though he was righting some awful, unknowable wrong done to him, and on the
other qualified indisputably as high sporting art.

I lived a shilling bus ride from Trent Bridge and on countless occasions I paid the
fare willingly for the privilege of watching him. Often with my grandfather I sat on

the front row of the George Parr stand, ate my packed lunch from its heavy grease-proof paper and drank dandelion and burdock from a tea flask.

My grandfather, after he scraped the Somme mud off his boots and returned from the scarring of the Great War, sought refuge in a quiet, uneventful life, which he partly found in the groomed greenery of the cricket field. He would talk about names that at first meant nothing to me: Hobbs, Hutton, Hammond, Sutcliffe.

Finally he spoke about Sobers. He did it in such a reverential way – the world record Test score, the six sixes, the label of the greatest ever allrounder – that Sobers struck me as a mythical figure, so perfect he could not possibly exist. I found it impossible to believe that this man was truly flesh; and, moreover, that I could catch the corporation bus to see him. When I did, it was love at first sight.

I was awed and slack-jawed at how easily runs came to him. Mind you, I quickly thought that everything came easily to Sobers, perhaps too easily. Occasionally the distracted slouch of his shoulders or the frustrated crease of his face betrayed that he was bored and needed to make the afternoon harder for himself by indulging in something unorthodox or risky, like a dare no one else would accept.

I saw him hit a six that rose no higher than four feet and thumped against the sight-screen like a military shell. It would have killed a whale. I saw him bowl whatever he liked – fast medium, orthodox slow left-arm and devious chinamen. I saw him take a balletic slip catch so effortlessly, the ball dropping bootstrap low and well wide of his right hand, that I do not know still how he reached it without stopping Time to get there. The liquid movement of his limbs captivated me.

With the bat he gave the impression of picking each delivery at least a full second before it was delivered, as though he got into position through psychic power as much as intuition and judgement. With the ball he could hold a game in the hard well of his palm and change it in an over.

He smiled and shook my hand and I felt as if I had been blessed

In memory I always see Sobers in high-definition: sharp, vivid, alive. He dominates my imagination to such an extent, and so overwhelmingly, that everyone around him is hazy and indistinct, like a photograph taken with a shaky hand. I was aware at once that he was a genius, unique and separate from the merely gifted, and I worshipped him because of it.

In the early 1970s he wore flannels with flares, which flapped enormously like the sails of a yacht. I bought a pair just like them. He used a Slazenger bat. I bought one of those too. He was sanguine but self-assured. I tried – and miserably failed – to copy that laid-back, cocky certitude. My bedroom walls were decorated with his black-and-white photograph, clipped from the pages of *The Cricketer*.

I longed to tell Sobers all this when I met him briefly two years ago. He had come to Leeds to make a speech. His joints were stiff now, his hair grey and his skin seamed with age. I did not care. Afterwards I waited in the long queue for his autograph, a nervous and besotted 11-year-old again. As he signed a picture and a miniature bat, I stuttered something lame and perfunctory about once living in Nottingham and admiring him. He smiled and shook my hand and I felt as if I had been blessed.

I said to his friend Basher Hassan, the old Notts opener who stood close by: "He was my boyhood hero." Basher replied: 'He's heard that one a few times.'" Yes, I wanted to say, but never with such heartfelt devotion.

DUNCAN HAMILTON is a journalist and author of two award-winning sports books: *Provided You Don't Kiss Me: 20 Years With Brian Clough* and *Harold Larwood: The Authorised Biography of the World's Fastest Bowler*

JOHN SNOW
by ALAN LEE

The vicar's son, the rebel and the poet

**John Snow's style and charisma were irresistible
to a young Alan Lee at Hove in the 1960s**

It started in the back garden, as all good cricket idolatry used to do. Innocent days, the early 1960s and there was no need for sophisticated computer games to transport a boy into the body of his hero – just a tennis ball, a strip of patio and a dustbin for stumps. Then the solitary dreamer could wheel away for hours, mimicking every bowler he had studied on TV until the repeated thumping of ball against bin brought either a parent or neighbour to boiling point.

I would have been 10 when I began shaping my run-up and delivery in hopeful, but no doubt hopeless, imitation of John Snow. And this was odd. Snow, at the time, was no more than a young tyro, uncapped by England. But two events had promoted him in my mind. One was the start of limited-overs cricket, the other a first visit to the ground I still love as no other.

'Snowie' would have been a godsend to 21st century cricket

Sussex won the first two Gillette Cups, largely because Ted Dexter, as captain, cottoned on quicker than most that tactics needed to be adjusted from the three-day norm. For me, still at junior school, it was a treat – an entire cricket match on TV in a day. And as that first final, against Worcestershire, in 1963 came to a thrilling climax, it was Snow and that lithe, flowing action, who caught my imagination.

A year later it took on sharper reality. We had family friends in Sussex and, unlike my own dear parents, these were sporting types. They took me to Hove and the intimacy of the place – virtually undimmed today – enchanted me. I sat on the boundary beneath the big scoreboard and the famous Sussex egg. When bad light intervened, I spotted Snow on the seats outside the pavilion. Summoning courage, I sprinted across the ground, up the steps and wordlessly thrust my virgin autograph book at him. Thankfully he did not refuse.

Sussex were my team from that moment on. Dexter and Jim Parks were heroes too and I bowed to no one in my admiration for the wiles of Ian Thomson. But the vicar's son from Worcestershire was just that bit more exciting – too exciting, as it turned out, for some of those who ran cricket at the time.

They took a while to pick Snow for England, maybe sensing the untamed side of his nature which he even conceded with the title of his autobiography, *Cricket Rebel*. The selectors overlooked him for the Lord's Test against West Indies in 1966, when I sat in the masses on the Grandstand balcony relishing my first taste of Caribbean banter. A week earlier, charging down the hill at Hove in righteous fury, Snow had taken 7 for 29 for Sussex against the touring side and then his Test career was properly launched.

'Snowie' would have been a godsend to 21st-century cricket. Unlike some current comparables, his charisma was not manufactured nor imported, it was just part of him. He even wrote poetry, for heaven's sake!

He would have had agents and commercial outlets bickering to acquire his services. And he would have loved it all. Well, apart from the modern training maybe. He never did like to overdo the training and I'm not sure all that sliding around the boundary would have appealed either.

Snow was 55 but the ball still fizzed past the batsman's nose

The closest he came to the cricket hotbed we now accept was by playing for Kerry Packer in the late 1970s. It was a no-brainer for Snow, whose Test career was virtually over as he entered his late 30s. Those trips in World Series Cricket also helped him into a post-playing career as a travel agent in which one of his faithful clients was yours truly.

It can rarely happen in life that a boyhood idol becomes an adult friend but it did to me. John not only fixed my flights and hotels when I covered England tours, he willingly presented his creaking limbs in media teams I organised each year. He loved the game, you see, loved it profoundly.

Snow turned up 10 Septembers in succession to play for me against a racing team at Findon and, in the mid-1990s, he turned out on the lovely riverside ground at Henley-on-Thames. Snow was 55 but, when a local batsman hit him for four, the glint returned to the eye and the next ball fizzed past the poor chap's nose. That competitive streak never left him.

There were bad times, of course – the brush with Sunil Gavaskar, various run-ins with the Sussex committee that made it all the more ironic he later became a member – but the good times outweighed them. Snow should have played many more than 49 Tests and finished with far more than 202 Test wickets. But there were those in power to whom he was never a hero.

At least he went out at Lord's as I would have planned he should, back in those childhood days. Against the 1975 Australians he dismissed Alan Turner and both Ian and Greg Chappell in a withering opening spell. The ground was in ferment as he retired to fine leg. "I bloody nearly cried," he later said. Up in the press box, I felt just the same.

ALAN LEE is horse-racing correspondent of *The Times*. He was the newspaper's cricket correspondent from 1988 to 1999

BRIAN STATHAM
by GILLIAN REYNOLDS

No Brylcreem or ballyhoo

Unpretentious and always happy to warn a batsman he was about to bowl a bouncer, Brian Statham's dignity won over Gillian Reynolds

I thought first of Denis Compton. I was so smitten with him when I was 12 that I kept a photo of him, cut out from the Brylcreem advertisement in the newspaper, under my desk lid. But was Compton, of Middlesex, Arsenal FC and England, really my favourite player or just my preferred Dad model? Difficult.

Then I thought of David Sheppard, magnificent cricketer, true gentleman, probably the best Bishop Liverpool has ever had, may (given the state of the Church of England) ever have. But was I thinking more of Bishop David's powerful work in the world

Heroic, in my book, doesn't mean being flash

"Accurate, determined": Statham bowls for England against Pakistan in 1962

and the city rather than David Sheppard, captain of Sussex and England? Hard to untangle the two because of the grace he brought to both.

So I knew it had to be Brian Statham, Lancashire fast bowler, one of the best in the history of the game, accurate, determined, consistent. In the days when he was in his full glory it always seemed to me he was being eclipsed by Fred Trueman and Frank Tyson. They got all the attention for being fiery and typhoonish. Statham got on with it, whether for Lancashire (including 13 seasons of 100 wickets) or England (252 Test wickets). Born in Gorton, one of Manchester's grimmer districts, in 1930, he died in leafier Stockport in 2000. His playing career began when he was 18, lasted 20 years, gave him a living if not much to live on afterwards. He was loved, respected, acknowledged. He was quiet. He was a hero.

Let us consider why people of my generation consider quietness to be a virtue. We know players today employ agents (press and otherwise) to make sure as much public noise as possible is made about them. We recognise that the making of such public show is logical. Cricket is sport and sport is business and business needs constant promotion. It is even desirable, since it may ensure that fewer great sportsmen face drastically reduced circumstances the minute their playing days are over. The annals of cricket are jammed with agonisingly true stories of past service unrewarded and only memories of summer triumphs past to see good family men through the long, hard, hard-up winters that followed. All the same, isn't there still a difference between just reward and constant ballyhoo? Or is that just because we grew up when a cricketer doing an advertisement for Brylcreem was as much ballyhoo as the general public found tolerable?

Which brings us to heroes. Heroic, in my book, doesn't mean being flash. It means doing what you do with strength and the will to win but doing so with grace, thought, care for others, being sportsmanlike. This attitude is not fashionable. Its very lack of fashion is what has finally put me off football. If you were brought up on Billy Liddell and Albert Stubbins you cannot warm to Wayne Rooney, wouldn't, even if he played for Liverpool (a possibility, I am glad to say, as remote as Mr Benítez turning to me for advice on the subject). Statham would actually warn players if he were about to bowl a bouncer. Yet he could bowl against South Africa at Lord's in 1955, take 7 for 39 and give England a victory no one could have predicted. That's heroic. It's also great sport.

Given, however, that current fashion favours the unsporting I have begun to fear for cricket. I could not believe the chaps on the radio before the final Ashes Test this summer, saying they were praying for rain. It's not what any hero, and not just of my variety either, would want. Imagine Brian Statham among the rain prayers. Or for that matter Fred Trueman, Frank Tyson, Denis Compton or David Sheppard. It's impossible.

Statham became full-time captain of Lancashire in 1965. He wasn't that good at it, they say. But he was still a beautiful bowler and a brilliant one. England called him back to play against South Africa in the last Test that same year. He took 5 for 40 in the first innings. He worked his socks off for Lancashire, right through to the end of his playing career and his two years (1995–97) as president.

I never saw him play except on television, when he made the news. Girls didn't go much to cricket then. I heard about him on the radio. I read what the *Manchester Guardian* and the *Liverpool Daily Post* said about him. I bridled whenever he was bowling with Trueman and Trueman got all the glory. He seemed to me quite like my other Lancastrian hero, Will Mossop, self-effacing boot-making genius in Harold Brighouse's great comedy Hobson's Choice. I followed whenever Statham was fielding because the radio said how brilliant he was. I worried whether he would ever get used to hot-weather tours. I didn't discuss this with anyone for fear of showing my ignorance of how he had developed from fast-medium to fast and why his style was not considered classical.

During his cricket lifetime I went from schoolgirl to wife to mother. I always loved his reputation for being easy-going, for getting on with everyone, for very, very seldom losing his temper. When John Brian Statham died in 2000, seven days short of his 70th birthday, the reaction from around the world showed he wasn't just my favourite, either.

GILLIAN REYNOLDS is radio critic of the *Daily Telegraph* and comes from Liverpool

County hero: Statham bowling for Lancashire against Surrey in 1960

CHRIS TAVARÉ
by GIDEON HAIGH

Minister of defence

**Chris Tavaré looked careworn at the crease from the moment he arrived.
But for Gideon Haigh that just added to the allure**

Some years ago I adjourned with a friend to a nearby schoolyard net for a recreational hit. On the way we exchanged philosophies of cricket and a few personal partialities. What, my friend asked, did I consider my favourite shot? "Easy," I replied ingenuously. "Back-foot defensive stroke."

My friend did a double-take and demanded a serious response. When I told him he had one, he scoffed: "You'll be telling me that Chris Tavaré's your favourite player next." My guilty hesitation gave me away. "You Poms!" he protested. "You all stick together."

Twenty-two years since Tavaré's only tour of Australia, mention of him still occasions winces and groans. Despite its continental lilt, his name translates into Australian as a very British brand of obduracy, that Trevor Baileyesque quality of making every ditch a last one. He is an unconventional adoption as a favourite cricketer, I admit, yet all the more reason to make him a personal choice.

> ## Tavaré did not score runs, he smuggled them out by stealth

Tavaré played 30 Tests for England between 1980 and 1984, adding a final cap five years later. He filled for much of that period the role of opening batsman, even though the bulk of his first-class career was spent at Nos. 3 and 4. He was, in that sense, a typical selection in a period of chronic English indecision and improvisation, filling a hole rather than commanding a place. But he tried – how he tried. Ranji once spoke of players who "went grey in the service of the game"; Tavaré, slim, round-shouldered, with a feint moustache, looked careworn and world-weary from the moment he graduated to international cricket.

In his second Test he existed almost five hours for 42; in his third, his 69 and 78 spanned nearly 12 hours. At the other end for not quite an hour and a half of the last was Ian Botham, who ransacked 118 while Tavaré pickpocketed 28. As an ersatz opening batsman Tavaré did not so much score runs as smuggle them out by stealth.

In the Madras Test at the start of 1982 he eked out 35 in nearly a day; in the Perth Test at the end of 1982 he endured almost eight hours for 89. At one stage of the latter innings he did not score for more than an hour.

Watching on television in the east of Australia, I was simultaneously aching for his next run and spellbound by Tavaré's trance-like absorption in his task. First came his pad, gingerly, hesitantly; then came the bat, laid alongside it, almost as furtively; with the completion of each prod would commence a circular perumbulation to leg to marshal his thoughts and his strength for the next challenge.

That tour, I learned later, had been a peculiarly tough one for Tavaré. An uxorious man, he had brought to Australia his wife Vanessa, despite her phobia about flying. Bob Willis, his captain, wrote in his diary: "He clearly lives every moment with her on a plane and comes off the flight exhausted. Add to that the fact that he finds Test cricket a great mental strain and his state of mind can be readily imagined." You did not have to imagine it; you could watch him bat it out of his system.

I saw us both as
aliens, maligned
and misunderstood

Tavaré could probably have done with a psychiatrist that summer; so could I. Our parallels were obvious in a cricket sense: I was a dour opening batsman, willing enough, but who also thought longingly of the freedoms available down the list. But I – born in England, growing up in Australia and destined to not feel quite at home in either place – also felt a curious personal kinship. I saw us both as aliens – maligned, misunderstood – doing our best in a harsh and sometimes hostile environment. The disdain my peers expressed for "the boring Pommy" only toughened my allegiance; it hardened to unbreakability after his 89 at Melbourne.

Batting, for once, in his accustomed slot at No. 3, Tavaré took his usual session to get settled but after lunch opened out boldly. He manhandled Bruce Yardley, who had hitherto bowled his offbreaks with impunity. He coolly asserted himself against the pace bowlers who had elsewhere given him such hurry. I have often hoped on behalf of cricketers, though never with such intensity as that day, and never afterwards have felt so validated. Even his failure to reach a hundred was somehow right: life, I was learning, never quite delivered all the goods. But occasionally – just occasionally – it offered something to keep you interested.

GIDEON HAIGH is Australia's leading cricket writer and the author of several books

"The boring Pommy": Tavaré faces Dennis Lillee at Old Trafford in the 1981 Ashes

SACHIN TENDULKAR
by GREG BAUM

The poster boy untouched by fame

Sachin Tendulkar has scored more Test runs than anyone. To Greg Baum, who has seen him stop trains in their tracks in India, he is the game's secular saint

The two keenest appreciations of Sachin Tendulkar were made from vantage points that could not have been more opposite and together serve as an incontrovertible cross-reference to his greatness.

The first was Sir Donald Bradman's famous remark to his wife during the 1996 World Cup that Tendulkar put him in mind of how he himself batted. The second is the widespread understanding in the cricket community that match-fixers did not bother to get on with their crooked business until Tendulkar was out; there is an anecdotal account of how Tendulkar once unknowingly ruined a fix by batting too blissfully well. It must be understood that neither reflection would have been made lightly. Sir Donald was not given to hyperbole or glibness. Nor would the fixers have bothered with throwaway lines.

Together, these tributes convey immutable impressions of Tendulkar that accord with less quantifiable, more aesthetic understandings of the glory of his batsmanship. Here is a man capable of changing the course of any game.

> ## He was born with extravagant talent but was also driven and indefatigable

Here is a man incorruptible in the face of the temptations that so many of his peers could not resist. Outside the laws or outside the off stump he could not be lured. Here is a man not susceptible to human failing in any endeavour; a man not so much invincible as invulnerable.

Here is a man whose name is synonymous with purity, of technique, philosophy and image. If Ian Botham was the Errol Flynn of cricket, or Viv Richards the Martin Luther King, or Shane Warne the Marilyn Monroe, or Muttiah Muralitharan the Hobbit, Tendulkar is surely the game's secular saint.

Right from the beginning, he appeared to be touched by divinity. He came among us as a boy-god, unannounced. He was 16 and was hit on the head in his first

appearance but neither flinched nor retreated a step. Nothing thenceforth could harm him, temporal or otherwise. He was short and stocky like all the best and mop-topped and guileless to behold. He has scarcely changed since.

Tendulkar was born with extravagant natural talent but he was also driven and indefatigable. He came not from another dimension, nor the mystical east, but like all greats from the nets. When a boy he would bat from dawn to dusk and even a little beyond. By such dedication he came to understand intimately his own gift and at length to lavish it upon others.

His movements at the crease are small but exact. He said once that he did not believe in footwork for its conventional purpose because the tempo of Test cricket did not permit a batsman the textbook indulgence of getting to the pitch of the ball. Rather he thought of footwork as a means of balancing himself up at the crease so that each shot was hit just as he meant it. He scores predominantly through the off side, unusual for such a heavy run-maker, but of course he can play every shot.

Tendulkar's method promotes an air of calm, reassurance and poise at the crease. Brian Lara's batting was characterised by explosion and violence, Steve Waugh's by grim resolve, Ricky Ponting's now by his energetic purpose; but Tendulkar's ways are timeless. His battles with Shane Warne, genius versus genius, were for the ages. It is said that the common element to concepts of beauty among all peoples and races is symmetry, a balance between all the parts. So it is with Tendulkar's batting.

He is not watching them but they are watching him. Still he stands tall

How easily he carries the hopes and takes responsibility for the well-being of untold millions on that impossible subcontinent; in this, too, he is divine. All eyes are upon him, day and night, but no scandal has attached itself in his private life or in his cricket endeavours. Across the land he is the little man on the big posters and hoardings, creating a kind of reverse Big Brother effect; he is not watching them but they are watching him. Still he stands tall.

Sometimes petty criticism is made that he fails India in its hours of need but it is not borne out by the figures. He has made more than 80 international centuries and is not done yet.

When called upon, he also bowls intelligently, if sparingly. He is sure in the field. There is even about him, as there was about many saints, something of the ingénu. He was not a natural captain for the modern era because he can lead only by example. He does not have a charismatic presence in a cricket stadium but fills it in a different way, as the one certainty in a sea of doubt. Batting is the most fraught of sporting pursuits because even for the best the end is only ever one ball away. Tendulkar seems to turn that verity upon itself.

As Tendulkar put Bradman in mind of himself, so he puts others in mind of Bradman. Once I was on a night train winding down from Simla to Kalka that stopped halfway for refreshments at a station lit by flaming torches. On a small television screen wreathed in cigarette smoke Tendulkar was batting in a match in Mumbai. No one moved or spoke or looked away. The train was delayed by 20 minutes. Not until Tendulkar was done could the world resume its normal time-tables and rhythms.

GREG BAUM is the chief sports writer for *The Age* in Melbourne

JEFF THOMSON
by JOHN BENAUD

Going out with a whang

John Benaud observed Thommo at close quarters but that did not dim his affection for the bowler with the ballet dancer's feet and a larrikin streak

My first memory of hero worship amounted to gross disloyalty. I was eight years old and, although the Australian Test team listed household names such as Arthur Morris, Lindsay Hassett, Neil Harvey, Ray Lindwall and Keith Miller (and my older brother Richie, although he was a rookie), in my dream matches on the front verandah, played with a ragged tennis ball and a cut-down bat, I was always the South African No. 3, Russell Endean. It was 1952, Jack Cheetham's team were visiting Australia and the Springboks, inspired as much as I was by Endean's prodigious run-gathering and electric catching, mugged Australia and drew a series the experts had said they would lose.

These days I wonder if I might have been guilty less of disloyalty than of an immature desire to offer good old Aussie 'fair go' to maligned visitors. Down under, the catch-cry of paying fans can sometimes be "We want a contest, not a walkover".

There was a good deal of well-meaning Aussie 'sympathy' in 1960–61 too. The late Frank Worrell's wonderful West Indians were on the receiving end of some harsh predictions, yet proceeded to lead brother Richie's team such a merry, memorable dance that it seemed every Aussie was cheering them from the rafters.

> "You've got to pick
> this bloke, he's the fastest
> I've ever faced"

Watched from afar, heroes can come and go as quickly as their halcyon summers; less fleeting is the fancy experienced when one is touched by genius.

Fast forward to the start of the 1970s. The scene is Bankstown Oval in the heart of Sydney's west; the outfield is dry and brown but there is a greenish tinge to the pitch. I am on strike with a full-size bat; the bowler, hard, shiny red ball in hand, is standing casually at the end of his run, about 40 yards away, and resembles any other knockabout Aussie bloke – skinny but sinewy, fair hair cropped close, eyes squinting in the bright midday sun.

His name is Jeff Thomson but his circling team-mates in their urgings simply call him 'Thommo'. While I am surveying the field, it is hard not to think of the latest Thommo rumour on grade cricket's grapevine: the previous weekend the former New South Wales opening batsman Warren Saunders, a champion exponent of the hook shot, was late on a Thommo bouncer. After being treated at hospital Saunders rang Neil Harvey, then a selector, and said: "You've got to pick this bloke, he's the fastest I've ever faced."

It certainly sharpens my focus. I had seen Saunders deal comfortably with Ray Lindwall and Wes Hall. I need a plan and the hook shot is not going to be part of it.

So Thommo begins – the high-stepping gait of a thoroughbred, bowling hand bobbing at waist level and the ball visible. It is conventional and comforting because facing a strange bowler for the first time invariably generates edginess. Then, in the split second before delivery, at gather, Thommo drags one leg behind the other in a sort of Swan Lake crossover, sways back and hides the ball behind his right knee – unconventional and very unsettling.

Upon achieving Test fame, Thommo was asked to explain this unique bowling method to a bunch of wide-eyed schoolboys. "I just run in and go whang," he said. I can vouch for that. On that day in Bankstown 'whang' meant a ball landing just short of a good length outside off, steepling past my unhelmeted head, up and over the wicketkeeper and one or two bounces into the fence for four byes.

In that instant I knew what Ian Chappell would confirm for the world's batsmen years later: you had 0.47sec to react once Thommo delivered. "It didn't allow you time to change your shot. If your first choice was wrong, you had to hope your luck was in," Chappell said.

"If those elite batsmen were not intimidated then body language is a flawed yardstick"

My favourite Thommo moment was in the Barbados Test of 1977–78, when I saw him tear into Gordon Greenidge, Desmond Haynes, Vivian Richards, Alvin Kallicharran and Clive Lloyd. If those elite batsmen were not intimidated by his pace and aggression, then body language is a flawed yardstick. Thommo took 6 for 77 off 13 overs in one innings. Think about that – a wicket every two overs.

He had an appeal for caught off the gloves rejected against Greenidge, probably because Greenidge rubbed his shoulder. At the end of play that day Thommo said: "That was gutsy, the way Gordon rubbed his shoulder, because his broken hand must have been hurting like hell."

We like our favourites alone on a pedestal. Wishful thinking abounds in Australia that Shaun Tait is 'another Thommo'. But Tait lacks that sliding foot-cross which enabled Thommo to maintain height at delivery and generate his extreme pace and lethal bounce. However, because technology rules this age of cricket, coaches might be able to create another Thommo. The good news for other Thommo fans, and batsmen, is: I've never seen a bowling machine with a larrikin streak.

JOHN BENAUD played three Tests for Australia, has been a Test selector and is currently a journalist. He is the author of *Matters of Choice: A Test Selector's Story*

FRED TRUEMAN
by SID WADDELL

Boys' own hero who became a mate

**Sid Waddell grew up worshipping Fred Trueman
and ended up working with him on television**

I became a fan of Frederick Sewards Trueman in the 1950s because he seemed to have jumped out from the pages of the boys' comics I devoured, with their tall tales of sporting derring do. Fred was cut from the same cloth as Wilson of the Wizard who, playing for Stoneshire at the age of 217, bowled a ball that smashed the sightscreen to smithereens. Like Fred, Wilson was well-muscled but lithe, the black hair chopped as if by a blind barber with a chin that jutted out like a chunk of granite.

There was no tradition of cricket in the Waddell mining family who lived in the Ashington area of east Northumberland. At school I was hopeless with the bat and wild with the ball. However, I was fast and a good thrower, so I made the 1st XI as a fielder. My dad Bob and I used to watch the Test matches on a flickering black- and-white telly with the curtains drawn. Bob, who had done every tough and dirty job in the pit and by the early 1950s was a specialist roof puller-down, had heard that Fred was of mining stock. "That Fred used to work as a putter down the pit, humping full tubs on and off the way. No wonder he's got shoulders like a dray horse," was my dad's opinion.

When I first met Fred at Yorkshire TV in 1972 he confirmed the view that putting was hard graft. He also told a typically wry story about what had happened to the tiny terrace cottage in the hamlet of Scotch Springs where he had been born. "No chance of me getting a blue plaque put up to honour me name. T'ouse were flattened to extend the bloody pit heap!"

> ## We roared him on
> ## so hard the steward's
> ## wife thought we were fighting

Watching Fred bowl on telly – hair flapping, brow knotted, shirt-tail dangling – made such a vivid impression on me during my first year at Cambridge University in 1959 that I tried cricket again. In the nets the skipper of the college casual XI said my bowling action was "just like Fred's" and so he opened with me against

Histon village. I spat, scowled, raced in and was hit all over the place by a young Popeye-armed oik called Ernie. I lasted one over.

Four years later I was in a working men's club in Geordieland watching England play West Indies at Edgbaston on telly. The place was full of miners, half of them 'black pint men' – lads still in their working muck having a jar before going home. I have never known an atmosphere like it: dozens of pints of Federation Special stood unsipped and cheese and pickles crozzled on trays as Fred put the Windies to the sword, taking 6 for 4 in 24 balls to win the match. As he sweated to eke ever more effort out of that mighty frame and bent his back to what John Arlott called "the cocked trigger", we roared him on so hard that the steward's wife thought we were fighting.

Fred Trueman and the Indoor League pub-games show were a match made in showbiz heaven and between 1972 and 1976 the show drew audiences of eight million. The support acts were arm-wrestlers and shove ha'penny players but the cream of the crop were Alan Evans, Leighton Rees and the darters. Fred, resplendent in wool cardy with suede panels and puffing a bendy pipe, was in his element. As producer of the show I was so chuffed the way the legend mingled with the tattooed, boozy giants of arrows.

But when it came to recording the links using an autocue, Fred was a disaster. It didn't help that he had just launched himself as a stand-up comedian at the Fiesta club in Stockton and celebrated a standing ovation till 3am. Seven hours, and three black coffees, later he faced the cameras. Imagine his shock when I walked in with an eight-pack of Newcy Brown.

"What's that, Sidney?" asked the great man, chops sagging in his pale face.

"Continuity," I replied. "You're drinking on tape and we have to match it."

He did his level best but was re-pissed by noon and we had to call it a day. But not before Fred felled us with laughter. He was just getting the hang of the autocue, when this line, about an arm-wrestler who dressed in tight leather, rolled: "Here he is Mark Sinclair-Scott, the Narcissus of the Knotted Knuckles." Due to a few blobs on the typing and Fred's fragile state, it came out as "the nancy boy with the knotted knuckles."

We looked out the window and there was Fred's mum humping a magnum of gin

Over the next three years he kept us entertained royally. He told me of how he and his boyhood mates got hold of hard balls for his bowling practice. "We'd go to the fair and I'd pay to chuck wooden balls at coconuts. First two goes I'd fling the balls right over the shy for my pals to collect. The bloke on the stall never twigged."

Mind you, FS was not the only character in the Trueman clan. My wife Irene and

I attended Fred's 50th birthday bash at his house at Gargrave. Fred's mum had a jar or two, then announced she was ready for home. "Tek a bottle home wi yer, mother," cried Fred. There was a clink from the kitchen and suddenly Fred looked out of the window. "Bloody Hell!" he cried. He raced out of the room. We looked out the window and there was this little woman humping a magnum of gin. Fred wrestled it from her and came back inside. "Gets a bit thirsty, me old mum," he said.

Fred rightly became a sporting legend but it was my privilege to know him as a good mate who never forgot his roots as a pit yacker.

SID WADDELL is the definitive voice of darts. His book *Bellies and Bullseyes: The Outrageous True Story of Darts* was short-listed in the 2008 British Sports Books Awards

VICTOR TRUMPER
by MARK RAY

Blithe spirit

The great Australian, with three shots for every ball, exemplified the freedoms of a more romantic age. Mark Ray remembers a dashing batsman and a generous man

Allan Border's 1989 Ashes tour was my first major assignment as a journalist. On the first day of the fifth Test at Trent Bridge, as Geoff Marsh and Mark Taylor were batting through to the close on the way to an opening stand of 329, a colleague and I, with our deadlines passed, decided to have a well-earned pint. As we chatted in the members' pavilion, I looked up at the row of old bats screwed on to the panelling above the bar.

There, in the centre, was a dark brown one with a metal plaque under it, which said it was Victor Trumper's bat from his legendary 1902 tour of England. On that trip Trumper made 11 first-class centuries, one of them in a single session of the Old Trafford Test. Admittedly the rest were made against lesser sides but, as ever with Trumper, it was the style that became part of the legend. Trumper entertained the English crowds and, as always, he won their hearts. He scored quickly and with flair, prompting Wisden to describe him as the best batsman in the world.

> Trumper was generous and charming to a fault – truly, a romantic figure

I had always been intrigued by the legend of the tall, dashing batsman who played with carefree grace. In the history books I read as a boy he was described as Australia's greatest batsman before Don Bradman. But it was the legend of the man that made him special. Bradman's legend was based on unbelievable statistics. He was the run machine par excellence. Trumper was the artist, the genius who cared more for his team-mates and his fans than for his place in the record books. Trumper's greatness could easily be missed during a look through the statistics but to read a biography was to be entranced.

Trumper was generous and charming to a fault, casual in dress, kind to children and greatly loved by opponents and team-mates – truly, a romantic figure. He ran a sports store in Sydney but was no great success. He was not hard enough, giving free equipment or discounts to people short of money. During his career there was a stand at the Sydney Cricket Ground called the Penny Stand – because entrance was a penny. Legend has it that Trumper would always arrive early and, with pockets full of enough loose change, walk over to the side of the ground opposite the dressing rooms to hand out pennies to poor boys hoping to get in. They came to expect Vic to give them a day at the famous ground to see their heroes in action.

Steve Waugh's love of his battered old baggy-green cap was inspired by Trumper's attitude to his Australian skull cap. He cherished it and never wanted a new one. To him the first was so precious that a replacement would not do. He was also celebrated for his casual approach to his playing clothes. Not for him the adage that if you cannot be a cricketer, you should at least look like one. After a day's play Trumper would roll up his cream trousers and drop them in his kitbag. The next morning he would simply unfurl them, put them on and head out. He was obviously interested in substance rather than appearance and I loved him for it.

He was tall and elegant, more Dravid than Tendulkar

One of the reasons Trumper's Test average ended below 40 was that he never sought easy runs. If the weather was fine and the pitch flat he usually threw his wicket away to give team-mates a chance to make runs. But, when the pitch was wet and treacherous, Trumper, as the senior batsman, would take full responsibility. This was not merely a whim. It is said that at New South Wales practice sessions he would slip the groundsman a shilling or two to prepare one wet wicket. After a net on a good pitch, he would go up to the end and practise on a sticky. I remember going to the same nets for a state squad practice session, looking to the far end and wondering if that was the strip the great Trumper used for his wet-weather practice.

Years earlier I was a teenager playing in the lower grades of Sydney club cricket. One day we played at Redfern Oval, a dustbowl of a ground ravaged by a winter of rugby league. Before play, as we inspected the unwelcoming pitch, a team-mate pointed to a window on the second storey of a building across the road, behind the sightscreen. He said it was the one Trumper broke with a straight drive about 60 years before. It was a big, big hit. The window had been left broken for years, in tribute to the great man. It had been repaired by the time I saw it. I think the building is still there.

I once saw some footage of Trumper batting. He is wearing a large white hat, looks tall and elegant – more the shape of Rahul Dravid than Sachin Tendulkar. He is facing a fast bowler and late-cuts him with aplomb, a classy, clever shot and exactly what you would expect from a batsman said to have had three shots for every ball.

The only other footage I have seen of Trumper is that of his funeral in 1915 at Waverley cemetery in the eastern suburbs of Sydney. Like so many Romantic heroes he died young, at 37, after a few years of sad, public decline. It is a hero's funeral, the horse-drawn hearse followed by dignitaries, and the parade watched by thousands of the fans who loved their Vic more than any other player.

If the mature Bradman stands for the ruthless pursuit of success which typifies modern Australian cricket, Trumper stands for the spirit of an earlier age, for a more carefree approach that put style and entertainment above results.

Every afternoon of that 1989 Test, my colleague and I had a ritual pint under his bat.

MARK RAY is an Australian first-class cricketer turned journalist. He has published several books, including two collections of his photographs

DOUG WALTERS
by KEVIN MITCHELL

You can tell by the way he walks . . .

**Doug Walters had a balanced view of batting, cricket and life in general.
That is why Kevin Mitchell likes him**

It is not because we share a first name or even that we grew up 30 miles apart. It is not because he was born on December 21 and I was born three days later. Nor is it because, at different times, we both played for the same junior club, run by the local police, on bouncy concrete wickets and under a blazing sun, in shorts and T-shirts and without cream or hat.

It is not because we were both in the ballot for National Service during the Vietnam war – he was drafted, I was not.

No, the reason Kevin Douglas Walters is my favourite cricketer is the way he walks.

You can tell a lot about people from their gait. Walters ambles, rolling on the outsides of his feet, ever so slightly bow-legged, back ram-rod straight, a man who knows where he is going but is in no particular hurry to get there. His is a country walk, not a city dash. It describes his balanced attitude to the game he was so good at.

And that is what we all loved about Doug. It was not that he did not care; anyone burdened with being called the new Bradman could hardly escape the responsibility of delivering on the talent given to him. But he did not care to the point where it changed him.

He was always the boy from Dungog. No doubt he still is.

It was inevitable growing up in the Hunter Valley of New South Wales in the 1950s and '60s that anyone addicted to cricket would regard Doug Walters as the champion of our times and attitudes.

Those were the days before car seat-belts and bicycle helmets, when it was OK to fall out of a tree and break your arm or go to the beach and get burnt to a crisp. They were times of unregulated fun.

And that is how Doug batted. In fact he was not a batsman to start with. From memory his days as a skinny kid in the Maitland and District Police Citizens Boys Club team were as a bowler who batted down the order.

Whatever he did, though, he did it brilliantly. When he did start to take his batting seriously, the runs flowed, not in a violent way but cleverly. Throughout his Test career Walters got his runs with deft placement and forceful hitting to all parts, pulling and cutting, the shots that live in the memories that we have of Bradman, too. Three times he got a hundred in a session in Tests, most memorably when he pulled Bob Willis for six off the last ball of the day at Perth.

"Obvious pleasures": Walters (right) plays cards
with Rick McCosker in the Edgbaston dressing room during the 1975 Ashes

It is said he lost some of his good years to the Army, called up in the mid-'60s when Australia's commitment to America's war in Vietnam was not the most popular game in town. He might have lost the chance to rack up some scores but I doubt the two years out blunted his skills at all.

There are several myths about Walters and one of them concerns his alleged nickname of that time, Hanoi. It was given him, it is said, because he was in Vietnam and used to get bombed every night. Well, Doug never went to Vietnam and his enthusiasm for beer was very much in its nursery stage then. Good story, though.

It says much about Walters that he takes in his country stride the conspiracy theory that he was drafted not because his number came up in the ballot but because he was a famous young sportsman whose presence in the Army would bolster the war effort.

He grew up in deferential times and was always respectful of authority – but only up to a point. Walters was one of the Australian team's best practical jokers and took delight in gently winding up po-faced officials.

His humour was not cruel, though. It was not in his nature but he did figure there was no point taking yourself too seriously.

Freddie (his real nickname, along with Bikki, the origins of which are tediously convoluted), indulged in all the obvious pleasures a young Australian male of his generation was brought up on. He drank, played cards, gambled on the horses – and still does.

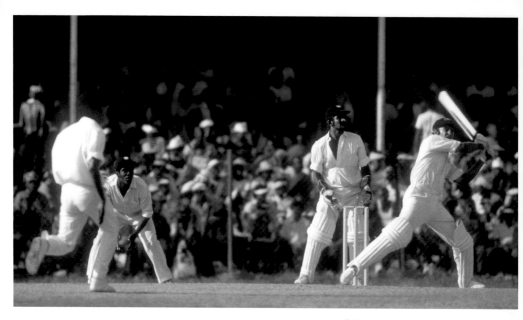

"The runs flowed": Walters on his way to a
hundred in a session against West Indies at Port-of-Spain in 1972–73

Famously, Doug drank 44 cans of beer on the flight from Sydney to London on the 1977 Ashes tour. It was regarded at the time as no more than harmless fun; in subsequent assaults on the record, though, the team management frowned on the practice.

It was not as if Freddie got outrageously drunk during that aerial lager marathon, though. As he said, and as friends will testify, he rarely got roaring drunk. Beer to Doug was something to be savoured quietly and over time. "I was always a bit of a sipper," he said.

It would be wrong to regard Walters as naïve – as anyone who has played cards with him would probably agree. He was quietly astute, undemonstrative but with a shrewd cricket brain.

His average of 48 was fine by him. He never mastered the moving ball on tours of England but was devastating against West Indies in conditions that suited his free hitting. Always a straight talker, he remarked once that players such as Steve Waugh cared too much about getting their average above 50. To Doug (and Steve's brother, Mark, a punting pal of Doug's), it was just a number.

Above all Walters was able to keep life in perspective. Maybe that is because he grew up in less complicated times. Whatever the reason, he had no problem articulating his philosophy.

"I enjoy life, mate," he said once. "I think you're dead a long while – that's what I was told and I haven't seen any proof of that not being right."

KEVIN MITCHELL writes for the *Observer Sport Monthly* and is a columnist for *The Wisden Cricketer*

Style and substance: during a century against England at Perth in 1974–75

ARTHUR WELLARD
by DAVID FOOT

Cock of the Somerset walk

David Foot holds a host of West Country characters in high affection but first among equals is Arthur Wellard of the mighty sixes, delivery leap and strolling sophistication

To someone embedded so incorrigibly in the ways, wonders and human oddities of West Country cricket over the decades the choice was one of wavering loyalties. It could have been Harold Gimblett for those instinctive, understated skills, Horace 'Nutty' Hazell for his jovial demeanour and evocative portly waistline, Reg Sinfield for his Tommy Trinder chin and battered boxer's nose or Bill Andrews, so often my confidant, who gave me gossip without a trace of malice. My affection was unbounded. But in the end I went for Arthur Wellard.

The earliest impressions never go away. I still see him strolling off the field at my hometown ground Yeovil in the late 1930s when Lancashire were the visitors. Winston Place and Eddie Paynter, names vaguely familiar to me, were playing but I did not notice them. It was Wellard I wanted to see up close. I ran across to the modest pavilion at the close of play. He was tall, manly, his dark hair greased back around the centre parting, thick, bronzed arms around the neck of a team-mate half his size. What a cricketer, I decided. I already knew he hit sixes and took wickets for a living.

That was my first sight of him. The second, again at a Yeovil ground, was at a Sunday benefit match. In the tea interval I anonymously patrolled the surrounds, in the hope of a fleeting moment of doting proximity. Then suddenly here he was, approaching me. No one else about. If only he would say: "Hello son, enjoying the cricket?" Anything, in fact. What he did say was: "Hey son, where's the bogs round hure?"

It was not the most romantic of conversational gambits. I stammered a response and pointed in the right direction. He thanked me and was on his way, no doubt to dispose of a little of the pre-match cheer. The voice, I discovered, carried the suggestion of regional vowels, acquired over the past 10 years or so after Kent had been tardy about signing him and Somerset found him digs in Weston-super-Mare.

Wellard was one of Somerset's greatest bowlers and only Farmer White took more wickets for them. He played in two Tests and would have gone to India in 1939 but for the war. My schoolboy contemporaries, like me, loved to ape his leap in the delivery stride. We collected the action pictures and chuckled over the way he seemed occasionally to tuck his left arm behind him at the same time as if scratching his back. In fact the action was orthodox. He consistently swung the ball away from the right-handers; his break-backs were renowned. Many of his

wickets came when he clean-bowled startled batsmen – just as well perhaps; too many catches went down ritualistically in the slips from the county's successive clutches of transitory amateurs.

On hot days he took
out his teeth when
stationed at silly mid-off

When, after the war, the limbs ached more, he turned to off-spin. There was still native cunning: after he had surreptitiously brought in another slip he would unexpectedly let go an old-style seamer. His fielding, full of sang-froid, was at times as comical as it was intrepid. On hot days he took out his teeth when stationed at silly mid-off. It changed his appearance considerably and, according to several of the pros, his improvised dentistry bordered on gamesmanship.

One of the county scorers worked out that a quarter of Wellard's runs came

One of Somerset's finest bowlers: Wellard against Surrey at The Oval in 1934

from sixes. He dispensed entertainment and there were groans when he was quickly out, not just from West Country crowds. His routine was to play back the first half a dozen deliveries with mannered coaching-school correctness. After that, whether the bowling was fast or slow, he aimed for the clouds. A succession of coaches encouraged him to hit straighter. Mostly they let him get on with it. That meant denting the Taunton tombstones or re-arranging groundsman Cecil Buttle's runner beans beside the car park.

Arthur, one felt, should have been a jokey extrovert. In fact, he was surprisingly laconic. The voice, when not inclining to Taunton and the Blackdowns, was more cockney than Man of Kent. "Come in a bit at cover, cock," he would say. Everyone was "cock". He got animated only when he went racing. That was something he did, perhaps a little too often on a Somerset pro's frugal salary.

Andrews idolised him "even though he always bowled with the wind behind him and I suffered at the other end". When the newcomer arrived from Kent, Bill was in awe of his appearance: his gaudy ties, check sports coats and pointed shoes. Not that Wellard was flashy but he carried an aura of self-contained sophistication. Yet he was basically an uncomplicated man. When it rained, he produced a pack

of cards. He left the majority of the professionals, fledglings when it came to poker
– or, more often, brag – out of pocket. Bill used to say: "He could remember the
position of every card in the pack – he was out of our class."

I was outraged
when Somerset chose
not to re-engage him

So he was in most cases when it came to cricket. In his first season for the county
he took 131 wickets. Three times he did the double. Twice at Wells he belted five
sixes in an over, scattering the dreamy young theological students seated at long-on.
Oldies claim he could hit the ball farther than Guy Earle and even Viv Richards.
Those who saw his hundreds at The Oval and Old Trafford would agree.

Everyone liked Arthur. That included Harold Pinter who wrote affectionately about
him and probably considered it a coup when Wellard agreed to play on occasions for
the playwright's XI. Like most of my fellow Somerset friends I was outraged when
Somerset chose in 1950 not to re-engage him.

DAVID FOOT has followed Somerset for more than 50 years and writes on cricket
for *The Guardian*

GRAEME WOOD
by CHRISTIAN RYAN

Hell was his home ground

Fearless, reckless and far from selfless, Graeme Wood brought a feverish edge to the game. Christian Ryan tells the story of the "strange one" the selectors rang when the Windies were in town

On a green and goose-bumped MCG wicket, some balls speared high and others shimmied low. Ian Healy, clobbered twice in the groin, felt sick. Dean Jones had a cracked rib and fingers so bruised it felt like he had been playing the piano for 10 hours. Seldom did Malcolm Marshall, Curtly Ambrose or Courtney Walsh land the ball in the batsman's half. Patrick Patterson, the brute, never did. "There is absolutely no pleasure in it," muttered Allan Border, no coward. "You walk in wondering where your next single is going to come from."

He was the man the selectors
called when the Windies
were in town

At this same hellhole, against these same hellraisers, Graeme Wood resembled a dartboard in pads. But if he was scared, he never flinched. If he was hurting, he did not grimace. He batted 130 minutes in the first innings and 50 in the second. He made 12 and 7. He never played for Australia again. It was Christmas 1988 and Christmas has felt a bit meaner, a bit thinner, ever since. Or it has to me.

The Test before that was at Perth, on a pitch chipped and crusty, littered with loose flakes of turf as big as pizzas. "No Test cricketer," wrote Mark Ray, "should have been asked to bat on such a pitch, let alone against West Indies." Wood jumped up and bunted down the screamers at his throat. The rest he hooked, pulled, cut, or drove. These were not simply shots out of a textbook but shots fired across Caribbean bows, executed with a tumbling back-lift and a loose flap of the arms. He made 111 and 42. One game before life's darkest injustice, this was cricket's brightest rearguard. Or it was to me.

Politicians must lie awake at night racked by visions of broken promises. Me, I often lie there wishing Woody's Test average was a few decimal points higher: 31.83 is such a slap in the face. Lower than Graeme Fowler and Haroon Rashid and Bevan Congdon.

It seems almost unspeakable. So belittling. Sometimes I wonder if he feels the same way.

As a teenager, the game was almost an afterthought for me: Graeme Wood came first, leather and wood second. When the Australians took a wicket I would scan the team huddle, looking for Wood – who he was next to, whether he was mates with DK and AB, one of the boys or a misfit. His bravery was part of the fascination. He'd wear a helmet but no grille. He'd field at short leg. He was the man the selectors rang when the Windies were in town.

Wood had a stance built to combat express bowling. Feet splayed wide apart, bum sticking out, so square-on that his front shoulder pointed almost to midwicket, as if daring the bowlers to aim at it – and when they did he would hook without hesitation, whether there was no man in the deep or three. Bouncers would be swayed rather than ducked, neck craned and eyes wide open, the ball grazing his moustache. They do not collate statistics about how often batsmen get cracked on the knuckles, but this is one table Wood might sit atop. A radio commentator once said his hands were stained violet and swollen to twice the size of a normal human's.

And yet this courage of Wood's was never selfless – not like his opening partner Bruce Laird's. Laird would do anything for his team. Wood, you fancied, would do anything to shore up his spot. If he made a duck in the first dig, you could tell he was trying extra hard in the second. If he made a hundred first-up, he'd lope out in the second innings like some obnoxious millionaire, serenely disinterested, then get out attempting something goofy. Only twice in 59 Tests did he make a half-century in each innings. Not an admirable record but never mind. Laird I always found a bit grey. Everything about Wood was utterly compelling.

Woody was a strange one, they'd say. Remote, self-absorbed, focused, disciplined

Before facing a ball he would gallop on the spot, pads and buckles flapping. He never played for the red ink, or calmly negotiated a maiden over. Everything had to be manic. He was dropped or recalled by Australia 14 times. So skittish was his running, lightning but hair-brained, that the papers called him "The Kamikaze Kid." He was run out four times in his first 22 Test innings, and there was always the sense that he was a bus crash waiting to happen. He once grafted 104 not out in an Adelaide one-dayer, against the hostile West Indians of course, but ruined it by running out Kepler Wessels, Wayne Phillips and Rod McCurdy. It was the first hundred by an Australian against West Indies in 27 one-day matches. Yet he wasn't even named man of the match. Why couldn't the world see what I saw?

Only one person, it seemed, shared my preoccupation with Wood; and that was the man himself. Old team-mates speak of an exquisitely gifted batsman, hard-working too, running pre-season laps with Olympian zeal, driven by his conviction that he could best serve the team by summoning the best out of himself. Woody was a strange one, they'd say. Remote, self-absorbed, focused, disciplined. Maybe he was too intense. Maybe to succeed in batting you need to realise how unimportant success in batting is.

But batsmen averaging in the mid-30s, 40s or 50s are dime a dozen. On reflection, 31.83 feels about right. If he averaged more, he would amount to less.

CHRISTIAN RYAN is a former editor of *Wisden Australia*. His first book *Golden Boy: Kim Hughes and the Bad Old Days of Australian Cricket* was published in 2009

DATE OF PUBLICATION

The articles in this book were taken from articles published in *The Wisden Cricketer* magazine in:

December 2007 (Wasim Akram); August 2008 (Mike Atherton); January 2008 (Ken Barrington); April 2008 (Bishan Bedi); May 2007 (Allan Border); 2006 (Geoff Boycott); February 2007 (Ally Brown); July 2007 (Brian Close); December 2005 (John Dye); June 2006 (Phil Edmonds); November 2005 (Farokh Engineer); January 2007 (Angus Fraser); February 2008 (Joel Garner); May 2009 (Adam Gilchrist); June 2007 (Graham Gooch); September 2008 (Darren Gough); July 2009 (David Gower); March 2005 (Tom Graveney); January 2009 (Wes Hall); November 2008 (Graeme Hick); June 2005 (Eric Hollies); April 2006 (Len Hutton); October 2005 (Douglas Jardine); August 2006 (Alan Knott); October 2007 (Allan Lamb); April 2005 (Harold Larwood); May 2008 (John Lever); October 2006 (Geoff Miller); September 2007 (Jim Parks); March 2006 (Graeme Pollock); July 2008 (Mike Procter); March 2008 (Clive Radley); February 2006 (Derek Randall); July 2005 (John Reid); September 2006 (Barry Richards); March 2009 (Garry Sobers); October 2008 (John Snow); January 2006 (Brian Statham); August 2005 (Chris Tavaré); December 2008 (Sachin Tendulkar); August 2007 (Jeff Thomson); November 2007 (Fred Trueman); September 2005 (Victor Trumper); August 2009 (Doug Walters); April 2007 (Arthur Wellard); May 2005 (Graeme Wood).

PHOTO ACKNOWLEDGEMENTS

The publishers would like to thank the following for permission to use their photographs:

Carl Sutton/Picture Post/Getty Images p.167 Fred Trueman; Central Press/Hulton Archive/ Getty Images pp. 10 Ken Barrington, 43–4 Farokh Engineer, 75 Wes Hall, 84 Eric Hollies, 88–9 Len Hutton, 90 Douglas Jardine, 92–3 Douglas Jardine, 102 Harold Larwood, 119 Graeme Pollock, 50–1, 53 Brian Statham, 179–80 Arthur Wellard; Dennis Oulds/Central Press/Hulton Archive/Getty Images: p.83 Eric Hollies; Edward Miller/Keystone/Getty Images (action) pp. 71, 73 Tom Graveney; Harrison/Topical Press Agency/Getty Images: p.135 John Reid; Hulton Archive/Getty Images: p.170 Victor Trumper; Joseph McKeown/Picture Post/Getty Images (portrait): p.71 Tom Graveney; Patrick Eagar: pp. 3 Wasim Akram, 8–9 Mike Atherton, 15, 17 Bishan Bedi, 18 Allan Border, 23 Geoff Boycott, 32 Brian Close, 36–7 John Dye, 38 Phil Edmonds, 46 Angus Fraser, 51, 53 Joel Garner, 55, 57 Adam Gilchrist, 58 Graham Gooch, 62 Darren Gough, 67–8 David Gower, 79, 81 Graeme Hick, 95 Alan Knott, 99 Allan Lamb, 108–9 John Lever, 111 Geoff Miller, 116–17 Jim Parks, 124–5 Mike Procter, 127 Clive Radley, 132–3 Derek Randall, 139 Barry Richards, 147 John Snow, 156–7 Chris Tavaré, 159 Sachin Tendulkar, 163 Jeff Thomson, 175–7 Doug Walters, 182 Graeme Wood; Titmuss/Getty Images: p.145 Garry Sobers.